EXECUTIVE SUMMARY

Although "small business owners" are often the subject of tax policy debate, a consensus does not exist regarding the specific attributes that distinguish small businesses from other firms. Previously, the Office of Tax Analysis had counted a small business owner as any individual who receives flow-through income from a sole proprietorship, partnership, S corporation, farming operation or miscellaneous rental activity. This overly broad definition was used because, for the majority of flow-through business income (partnerships and S corporations), it was not possible to trace income from the business entity to the respective owner(s). Due to newly accessible tax data, this technical constraint has been overcome. In this paper, we present a methodology that utilizes these new tax data, thereby allowing a more nuanced definition of small business owner.

Our revised methodology begins with the characteristics that define a "business." We look at the six tax forms and schedules filed by individuals or firms that could potentially represent business activity: Form 1040 Schedules C, E and F, Forms 1065, 1120 and 1120S. We develop two tests based on income and deductions reported on those forms and schedules to separate filers into business and non-business groups. We then further sub-divide our business group into small and other businesses. Drawing from various tax code provisions that provide preferential treatment to certain filers, we set the small business threshold at $10 million of income or deductions. Using these criteria, we find that 54 percent of taxpayers who file one of the six forms or schedules we consider qualify as both a business and a small business for tax year 2007. Those small businesses reported approximately 17 percent of total and net business income. We also find that slightly more than one-fifth of small businesses conform to our definition of an employer.

Once we set the parameters that define a small business, we then use newly accessible tax data to separate small business income reported on the individual income tax return from other (i.e., non-small) business income. In this manner, we identify relevant characteristics of small business owners such as reported Adjusted Gross Income (AGI) and applicable marginal tax rates. For tax year 2007, our previous methodology counted 34.7 million filers reporting $662 billion of net flow-through business income as small business owners. Using our revised methodology, we count 20.0 million filers reporting $376 billion of net business income as small business owners under a broad measure of small business owner. Under our narrow definition, we count 9.4 million filers reporting $335 billion of net business income as small business owners.

Because it excludes large businesses, our revised methodology also affects the distribution of net business income across AGI classes for small business owners. Using our previous methodology, eight percent of small business owners reporting 75 percent of net flow-through business income had AGI above $200,000. Using our revised methodology and our broad definition of small business owner, those shares are 11 and 64 percent respectively. Under our narrow definition, those shares are eight and 57 percent respectively.

We note that our revised methodology is but one reasonable approach that could be used to identify small businesses and their owners. However, we believe it represents a significant improvement over previous methodologies that were constrained by data limitations.

1

I.   Introduction

Policymakers often inquire about the tax code's impact on "small business" and "small business owners." Although many factors motivate their concerns, two factors seem especially relevant. First, it is widely believed that many small businesses operate at a competitive disadvantage relative to their larger counterparts. For example, small firms might have greater difficulty raising the capital necessary for investment and expansion. They might also realize thinner profit margins if their sales volume is insufficient to exploit economies of scale. Second, despite any inherent disadvantages, small businesses are perceived to generate a disproportionate share of overall economic and employment growth. For these reasons, policymakers are concerned that the tax code not excessively burden small businesses or their owners.

Currently, a consensus does not exist regarding the specific attributes that distinguish small businesses from other firms. Previous analyses by the Office of Tax Analysis (OTA) and others (e.g., Joint Committee on Taxation, Tax Policy Center) counted a small business owner as any individual who reports flow-through income from a sole proprietorship, partnership, S corporation, farming operation or miscellaneous rental activities. Although this approach is easily implemented and understood, it is at once too broad and too narrow. The approach is too broad because it includes owners of large firms as well as individuals whose business income is negligible or who might not be engaged in canonical business activities. The approach is too narrow because it excludes owners of small C corporations. Due to these shortcomings, previous analyses of how tax law changes impact "small businesses" or "small business owners" have not been as informative as they might have been – the analysis might not address the true underlying concerns of policymakers. For example, should we count all misclassified employees and independent contractors who file a Schedule C (sole proprietorship) as small business owners? Should we count partners of large hedge funds as small business owners? Although issues such as these have been noted in the past, to date there has been no effort to address them in a satisfactory manner.

In this paper, we describe a methodology to define a business, a small business, and a small business owner using tax return data. The methodology begins with the six tax forms and schedules filed by individuals or firms that could potentially represent business activity. We separate those returns into business and non-business groups, and then further sub-divide the business group into small and other businesses. The final part of our methodology uses newly accessible tax data to link income reported by small businesses to the individual income tax return of their respective owners. In this manner, we identify relevant characteristics of small business owners such as adjusted gross income (AGI) and marginal tax rates.

This technical paper has a narrow focus, so it does not discuss the myriad tax-related issues that affect small businesses and their owners.[1] Nor does it compare the definitions used in this paper to those used by other governmental agencies, such as the Small Business Administration (SBA). In general, the small business definition used by Treasury and the SBA will differ because they are based on different

---

[1] For a discussion of these issues, see, for example, Gary Guenther, CRS Report, February 26, 2010, "Distribution of Small Business Ownership and Income by Individual Rates and Selected Policy Issues"; Jane Gravelle, CRS Report, September 3, 2010, "Small Business and the Expiration of the 2001 Tax Rate Reductions: Economic Issues"; Alan Viard & Kevin Hassett, "The Small Business Tax Hike and the 97% Fallacy," Wall Street Journal, September 3, 2010; Haltwinger, Jarmin & Miranda, "Who Creates Jobs? Small vs. Large vs. Young," NBER Working Paper No. 16300, August 2010.

data sources and concepts and are used for different purposes. The definitions used by SBA identify firms that are eligible to receive certain government grants and assistance and is generally considered to be a relatively broad measure.[2] By contrast, the small business definition we employ draws on tax code provisions that provide favorable treatment to firms that fall under various size thresholds.

Although we identify certain taxpayers as small business owners, we do not assert that those individuals are necessarily engaged in entrepreneurial activity. The Meriam-Webster dictionary defines an entrepreneur as a person who organizes, manages and assumes the risk of a business or enterprise. The individuals we identify as small business owners may or may not actively participate in an enterprise, and may incur little or no risk. We also note that our methodology likely excludes some individuals who might be viewed as entrepreneurs because their business tax return does not conform to our definition of a small business.

Finally, we note that our methodology is but one approach that could be used to identify small businesses and their owners. Although many different approaches could be used for this purpose, the issues we discuss would remain pertinent and must be addressed (either implicitly or explicitly) regardless of the methodology employed. Hence, this technical paper serves a dual purpose: (1) to correct known shortcomings of previous methodologies and (2) to discuss issues that policymakers should clarify to ensure that analysts use appropriate data to evaluate current and proposed tax policy.

This technical paper proceeds as follows. Section II discusses the criteria we use to distinguish business from non-business entities. In Section III, we further sub-divide businesses into small and other entities and provide tabulations for small businesses based on total income, net income, industry, and employer status. Section IV discusses the methodology we use to identify the individual income tax returns of small business owners. It presents tabulations of small business owners based on AGI and marginal tax rate. Section V concludes our analysis with a review and summary of our findings.

II.   Business versus Non-Business Filers

Our analysis begins with all entities that file one or more of the following business tax returns: Form 1040 Schedules C, E-Part I, and F (sole proprietor, miscellaneous rental real estate income, and farmers), Form 1065 (partnership), Form 1120 (C corporation), and Form 1120S (S corporation).[3] Although we refer to these forms and schedules as "business" returns, closer inspection reveals that many filers are not engaged in business activity as it is traditionally understood. Some examples of non-business activity include the following:

---

[2] To identify small firms eligible for its programs, the SBA uses industry-specific size standards that are based on sales or number of employees. If based on sales, the threshold ranges from just under $1 million to $35.5 million, but most industries employ the $7 million benchmark level. If based on number of employees (capital intensive industries), employment levels range from 50 to 1,500 employees, but most industries employ the 500 employee benchmark level. For research purposes, the SBA generally uses firms with fewer than 500 employees. See http://www.sba.gov/advo/research..

[3] If an individual reports income that is attributable to multiple types of business entities, then we do not combine the activity to form a single business entity. For example, it is not uncommon for taxpayers to report income from an S corporation and a sole proprietorship. However, we do combine multiple filings of Schedule C or Schedule F by an individual to form a single entity of each type. In general, the combination of activity reported on multiple Schedule C filings increases the likelihood that an individual will be classified as a small business owner.

- Many Schedule C filers work for one or more firms and receive 1099-MISC forms that report their "non-employee compensation" instead of W-2s that report wages. These individuals report this compensation as gross receipts (per the instructions) and often report no deductions, or very minimal deductions that reflect elements of personal and business use, such as transportation, travel or meal expenses. Some of these filers are technically misclassified employees; others are correctly treated as independent contractors.[4] In many instances, these individuals are not substantially different than employees of the firm to whom they provide labor services.
- Individuals or entities might form partnerships to re-distribute earnings that are passed through from other partnerships. These entities are conduits that merely redistribute funds. Other partnerships might solely hold financial assets and receive interest, dividends or capital gains but conduct no business activity. These partnerships could be considered "passive investment vehicles."
- Certain C corporations could also be viewed as investment vehicles if they merely hold investments and conduct little or no business activity. Individuals could benefit from the graduated corporate rate structure (such as 15 or 25 percent) and minimize tax liability by remitting tax at the lower corporate rate and then retaining earnings in the corporation.[5]
- Certain individuals who file Form 1040 Schedule E, Part 1 might report minimal income due to the incidental rental of a vacation home.
- Individuals might attempt to claim a tax loss for activity that is properly characterized as a hobby, not a business.

The first step in our revised methodology is the development of criteria to separate business from non-business entities. To do this, we look to the tax code. Despite the stylized examples above, the distinction between business and non-business activity is not always clear, and the Internal Revenue Code (IRC) fails to provide explicit guidance because it does not define the term "trade or business." In general, the IRC characterizes most activities carried on for a livelihood or for profit as a trade or business. If a taxpayer is engaged in a trade or business, then the taxpayer may deduct from gross income all "ordinary and necessary" expenses of carrying on the trade or business that are paid or incurred during the tax year.[6] If there is uncertainty about whether an activity qualifies as a trade or business, then tax authorities will apply certain tests and consider the relevant facts and circumstances of individual taxpayers. This approach is referred to as the "hobby loss rules." If an activity is deemed a hobby, and not a trade or business, then expense deductions are limited to the income produced by the activity so that hobby losses cannot offset other income. By contrast, there are no restrictions on active trade or business losses; they may be used to offset all other types of income, regardless of its source.[7]

---

[4] For discussion of legal distinctions between misclassified employees and independent contractors, see, for example, the Administration's FY12 Budget proposal, "Increase Certainty with Respect to Worker Classification." "Worker classification generally is based on a common-law test for determining whether an employment relationship exists. The main determinant is whether the service recipient (employer) has the right to control not only the result of the worker's services but also the means by which the worker accomplishes that result." Department of the Treasury, February 2011, "General Explanations of the Administration's Fiscal Year 2012 Revenue Proposals," p. 107. See http://www.treasury.gov/resource-center/tax-policy/Documents/Final%20Greenbook%20Feb%202012.pdf .

[5] Some such corporations might be subject to the personal holding company tax.

[6] An expense is "necessary" if it is appropriate and helpful to the taxpayer's business. An expense is "ordinary" if it is one that is common and accepted in the particular business activity.

[7] Because of the passive activity loss rules, some taxpayers may not be able to deduct certain losses from trade or business activities in which they do not "materially participate."

In order to distinguish hobby from business (i.e, for-profit) activities, tax authorities rely first on the historical profits test from IRC Section 183(d). This test states that, in general, an activity is presumed to be engaged in for profit if gross income from the activity exceeds the deductions attributable to such activity in any three of five consecutive tax years, including the current tax year. If an activity fails the historical profits test or the test is not applicable, then Section 1.183-2 of the Income Tax Regulations lists nine specific factors that may be used to distinguish business from hobby activity. They are as follows:

- The manner in which the taxpayer carries on the activity.
  - Was it a businesslike manner? Did the taxpayer keep accurate books and records?
- The expertise of the taxpayer.
  - Did the taxpayer prepare for the activity through the study of accepted business, economic, and scientific practices? Did the taxpayer consult with experts?
- The time and effort expended by the taxpayer in carrying on the activity. Was it "substantial"?
- An expectation that assets used in the activity may appreciate in value.
- The success of the taxpayer in carrying on other similar or dissimilar activities.
- The taxpayer's history of income or losses with respect to the activity.
- The amount of occasional profits, if any, which are earned.
  - The amount of profits in relation to the amount of losses incurred, and in relation to the amount of the taxpayer's investment and the value of the assets used in the activity, may provide useful criteria in determining the taxpayer's intent.
- The financial status of the taxpayer. Does the taxpayer have other sources of income?
- Elements of personal pleasure or recreation.

We condense these nine factors into two general principles that we use to determine whether activity reported on business tax returns reflects "substantial" operations that are carried out in a "businesslike" manner. They are as follows:
- De Minimis Activity. Does the activity generate, or have the potential to generate, income that is non-negligible to the business owner(s)? Under this principle, very small entities would not qualify as a business, even though they may report income and deductions on the business return. For example, an individual who reports small amounts of rental income and expense on Schedule E from a two-month rental of a vacation home might not qualify as a business.
- Businesslike Activity. If the income is non-negligible, do the owners undertake actions that demonstrate "businesslike" activity? If they do, then they should report expenses related to employees, inventories, investment, office supplies, utilities, insurance or rent. Under this principle, Form 1040 Schedule C filers who report only their own labor compensation as gross receipts (e.g., certain service providers), but little or no expenses, would not qualify as business entities because most of those filers are not substantially different than employees of the firm who earn and report wage income. Entities that merely redistribute income or function as investment vehicles would also not qualify as business entities.

We convert these principles into two tests that we apply to all potential business returns. If an entity passes both tests, then we deem the entity a business. The two tests are as follows:

De Minimis Test: Total income or total deductions exceed $10,000, or their sum exceeds $15,000.

Receiving income and incurring expenses can signal business activity. We apply our first test to income and deductions (or their sum) reported on the tax return to allow symmetric treatment of business activity. We eliminate entities that fail this test because the reported activity, regardless of its form or nature, does not generate substantial income to the owner(s) and it is unlikely that the activity required significant time and effort on the part of the owner(s). This test also eliminates many filers who are likely engaged in hobby activities.

We define total income as the sum of all income reported on the business return including gross receipts, rents, dividends, capital gains, royalties, and interest.[8] [9] If an income source can be negative (e.g., a loss from the sale of business assets), then we use the absolute value so that it does not offset other types of income and because negative amounts also represent business activity. The definition of total deductions is discussed below.

Business Activity Test: Total deductions exceed $5,000.
Our second test eliminates entities that only report income, with minimal or no deductions, such as pure labor providers or investment vehicles. The deduction floor we impose ensures that entities deemed a business operate in a "businesslike" manner through minimal outlays for investment (depreciation expenses), the carrying of inventories (cost of goods sold), employment of individuals, rents for buildings or equipment, or payments to other firms for goods or services. More broadly, the deduction floor generally requires that business income reflect more than a pure return to labor services provided by the owner(s). This requirement seems to reflect the intention of policymakers. When tax code provisions provide preferential treatment to small businesses, the provisions usually target expenses such as equipment investment (e.g., Section 179 expensing), cost of goods sold (e.g., exceptions to inventory accounting), and start-up costs. Preferential treatment is not targeted towards individuals who provide only labor services. Those individuals generally do not benefit from provisions targeted to small businesses in the tax code.

For the purposes of our tests, we define total deductions as the sum of wages-salaries, interest paid, payments for goods and services purchased from other firms, rents, repairs, taxes, advertising, bad debts, depletion, depreciation, and other miscellaneous deductions reported by the entity. For corporations, we do not include payments for "compensation of officers" (line 12, Form 1120 or 1120S) because it is likely that those deductions represent the "reasonable compensation" that owners are required to pay themselves for labor services provided to the firm.[10] [11] By excluding those deductions, we place corporations on equal footing with partnerships and sole proprietors. (General partners and sole proprietors do not report payments to themselves for services provided to the firm as a wage expense. All returns to labor and capital are included in residual profits and are subject to self-employment taxes.)

---

[8] For partnerships and S corporations, we include any gross rents reported on Form 8825, which partnerships and S corporations engaged primarily in rental real estate activity must file. Firms report gross rents plus any associated deductions on that form. Any net income is then carried over to the Schedule K submitted with Form 1065 (partnership) or 1120S (S corporation). We also include all other income and deduction items reported by those entities on Schedule K.

[9] For the income test, we exclude any miscellaneous "other income" reported on the front page of business returns because that field may include amounts that are not properly viewed as income, such as refunds of federal and state fuel taxes (farmers and sole proprietors) or income passed through from partnerships that we already count (corporations).

[10] If a corporation reports only payments for compensation of officers and no wages paid to employees, then we also disregard any deductions for employee benefit plans (generally health) and pension-profit sharing plans since those benefits likely accrue to the owner(s).

[11] For partnerships, we exclude guaranteed payments to partners (line 10, Form 1065) for similar reasons.

We must observe deductions besides wage payments to corporate owners to consider an entity a business.

We make one further adjustment to this test in cases where the sum of gross receipts and rents comprise less than ten percent of total income. In those cases, the entity essentially reports investment income only. To ensure those entities are not merely passive investment vehicles, we exclude interest expense from total deductions. Our tests would deem an entity that reports $50,000 of interest income and $20,000 of interest expense as a "non-business." For entities that primarily report investment income, we must observe other deductions besides interest expense to deem the entity a business.

Note on Self-Employed Individuals

Due to the thresholds we apply for our business tests, we include some and exclude other self-employed individuals from our business group. While it seems clear that individuals who report only income and no deductions might not be engaged in business activity as typically conceived (e.g., misclassified employees, certain independent contractors), it is less clear at what point those same individuals engage in sufficient "businesslike" activity as evidenced by deductions and become business entities. For the purposes of this paper, we have set that threshold at $5,000. As we discuss in the next section, lowering that threshold does not alter our basic results and conclusions; it merely increases the number of very small business entities, most of whom are self-employed individuals.

We apply the same business tests to self-employed individuals as applied to other businesses that employ individuals and have a separate business identity. Under our tests, an individual who earns a livelihood as a painter and reports $40,000 of income and $6,000 of supplies would qualify as a business entity and small business owner. An individual who sub-contracts as a consultant and reports $80,000 of income and $9,000 of related expenses would also qualify as a business entity. However, in either case, if reported deductions fell below $5,000, then our tests would not deem the self-employed individual a business entity.

Results: Business vs. Non-Business Entities by Return Type

The data used for this analysis are from the IRS Statistics of Income (SOI) individual and business tax files for tax year 2007. All tax files are stratified random samples weighted to represent national totals. For Schedules C, E, and F, the file contains roughly 325,000 individual income tax returns. Data for partnerships are from a sample of roughly 39,900 tax returns, while the S corporation sample includes 34,000 returns and the C corporation sample includes 61,600 returns.[12] Table 1 presents data for all filers across the six business returns we examine, and results from the application of our two business tests. Results are as follows:

Form 1040, Schedule C: Sole Proprietors

---

[12] For detailed discussion of the data and sample characteristics for individual tax returns, see *Statistics of Income: Individual Income Tax Returns 2007*, Publication 1304 (Rev. 07-2009), Internal Revenue Service, Department of the Treasury. Because of the sample construction, varying degrees of representation and potential error (relative to the population) are present across sample strata. For example, for Schedule C filers the sample fully represents the population for the highest income strata (for "$5 million under $10 million" and "$10 million or more"); at the lower income levels of under $30,000, a sample of 12,426 represents nearly 10 million returns of the population.

Individuals who file Schedule C may be engaged in a wide range of activities. While some filers operate businesses that provide their sole means of support, other filers report incidental activity in which they are engaged on a part-time or seasonal basis. Many filers do not operate a business, but rather supply labor or services to a firm in exchange for remuneration on an hourly or per-job basis. For this final group, the deductions they report may not represent outlays that need to be recouped via future sales of goods and services, but rather are expenses that will be quickly reimbursed by the firm that employs the individual. For example, a firm might pay a service provider a higher hourly wage than a comparable employee as reimbursement for travel expenses. Alternatively, a firm might directly reimburse a service provider if an itemized bill is presented for the same expenses. Regardless of the reimbursement method, the individual would report all remuneration as gross receipts on Schedule C, as well as any deductions associated with the provision of labor services. Common deductions for these filers are transportation and travel-meal expenses.

In the situation just described, the individual may not be substantially different than an employee of the firm from which he or she receives compensation. Yet, at some point, these same individuals could also be considered a small business entity to the extent they do more than merely supply labor services. For example, the individual might also incur expenses related to inventories, advertising, office supplies, and the payment of utilities or rent. Those types of deductions provide a strong signal that the individual engages in businesslike activities such as itemizing and tracking expenses, the development of a business plan or the maintenance of a separate business address.

Because many Schedule C filers could be viewed as quasi-employees of the firms to whom they provide labor or services, we discount, but do not disregard, certain deductions that are claimed intensively by those individuals: car-truck expenses (line 9, includes the standard mileage deduction) and travel, meals and entertainment (line 24).[13] We discount those deductions by 50 percent because (1) they are claimed intensively by misclassified employees and independent contractors, (2) they are potentially a weaker signal of business activity and (3) it is likely that many of those deductions contain both personal and business elements. Therefore, if a Schedule C filer reports $3,000 of advertising expenses and $8,000 of car-truck expenses, then we set total deductions equal to $7,000.[14]

For tax year 2007, 23.2 million individuals filed a Schedule C, and 10.7 million (46 percent of total) qualify as a business based on our tests (see Table 1). Although we deem less than one-half of filers a business, those entities reported the vast majority of total income (94 percent, average income of $120,200) and net income (80 percent, average profit of $20,900). The proportion of filers that were profitable is the same for our business group (74 percent) compared to all Schedule C filers.

The application of our two business tests eliminates 12.5 million Schedule C filers from our business group. Of the filers we exclude: 10.2 million filers failed the *de minimis* test and 2.3 million filers reported insufficient deductions to pass our second business test. The filers we exclude reported an average of $7,000 of total income and $4,600 of net income.[15]

---

[13] For detailed instructions regarding the amounts that filers may claim for these expenses, see IRS Publication 463: Travel, Entertainment, Gift and Car Expenses.

[14] This additional restriction eliminates approximately 700,000 Schedule C filers from our business group. Those filers reported average Schedule C total income of $15,800 and average net income of $7,900.

[15] There is substantial overlap between our two business tests. Many filers eliminated under the *de minimis* test would also be eliminated under our second business test.

Table 2 provides additional detail regarding the sole proprietors we exclude from our business group based on total income reported on Schedule C. Most of these filers (81 percent) reported less than $10,000 of total income on Schedule C. Across all filers, Schedule C net income comprised only seven percent of Adjusted Gross Income (AGI) reported on Form 1040 (final column), suggesting that Schedule C business income was not significant for most filers we exclude. By comparison, wages and salaries comprised two-thirds of AGI and investment income comprised 22 percent of AGI (interest, dividends or capital gains, not shown in table). Although we exclude filers based on Schedule C income and deductions, 1.1 million filers reported $45 billion of rental, partnership or S corporation income on Schedule E. Given the average level of Schedule E income reported by these filers ($39,500), it is likely that most of the rental operations, partnerships or S corporations owned by those individuals will be included in our small business group, and their owners will ultimately be included in our tabulations of small business owners.

Form 1040, Schedule E: Supplemental Income and Loss (Part 1), Rental Income
Taxpayers report rental real estate activity on Part 1 of Form 1040, Schedule E.[16] Unless the owner provides "substantial" services to the tenants or qualifies as a real estate professional, the IRS generally considers activity reported in Part 1 of Schedule E as a passive activity for the purposes of the passive activity loss rules. Therefore, taxpayers might face limitations on their use of losses attributable to such activity. Despite this treatment, we deem rental activity a business if it passes our tests because, much like a traditional business, the owners provide services (housing) to consumers (tenants). In that capacity, owners incur and report various business expenses, such as advertising, insurance, interest, repairs, and cleaning and maintenance.

However, in many cases, rental activity may not denote the conduct of an active trade or business. The rental activity may be incidental to personal use, or may not differ substantially from an investment in a financial asset, such as when an owner reports no expenses besides those associated with holding title to the property (i.e., mortgage interest, property taxes, and depreciation). Similar to our treatment of partnerships and corporations that invest in financial assets, we require that Schedule E rental filers evidence at least minimal active management of the property beyond deductions for mortgage interest, property taxes and depreciation. To ensure that individuals reporting rental income engage in minimal businesslike activity, we exclude depreciation and mortgage interest expenses from computed deductions.[17] We require that owners report other types of expenses such as cleaning, advertising, maintenance or repairs that suggest active management of the properties.

For tax year 2007, 9.6 million individuals reported rental income on Part 1 of Schedule E, and reported total income of $255 billion (average income of $26,500) and net income of -$18 billion (average loss of -$1,800). The 4.6 million (48 percent of total) filers we deem a business reported total income of $212 billion (average income of $46,200) and net income of -$22 billion (average loss of -$4,800). The proportion of filers that were profitable is slightly lower for our business group (35 percent) compared to all filers (42 percent).

---

[16] Royalty payments are also reported on Schedule E, Part 1. We do not include royalty income in our analysis because the income could represent compensation attributable to activity many years removed.
[17] The data do not itemize property taxes separately.

The application of our two business tests eliminates 5.0 million Schedule E rental filers from our business group. Of the filers we exclude: 3.9 million filers failed our first *de minimis* business test and 1.1 million filers reported insufficient deductions. The filers we exclude reported an average of $8,400 of total income and $800 of net income.

Form 1040, Schedule F: Profit or Loss from Farming
When applying our business tests to farm income, we include income and expenses reported on Form 1040, Schedule F and Form 4835, Farm Rental Income and Expenses. Individuals use Form 4835 to report farm rental income based on crops or livestock produced by a tenant if they were the landowner (or sub-lessor) and did not materially participate in the operation or management of the farm. For the purpose of our business tests, we include any income from cooperative distributions, commodity credit corporation loans, and crop insurance proceeds in our definition of total income.

For tax year 2007, 2.5 million individuals filed a Schedule F, a Form 4835, or both. Those filers reported total income of $134 billion (average income of $53,300, predominately sales of livestock or agricultural products) and -$13 billion of net income (average loss of -$5,300). The 1.4 million filers (56 percent of total) we deem a business reported total income of $130 billion (average income of $92,200) and net income of -$13 billion (average loss of -$9,200). The proportion of filers that were profitable is slightly lower for our business group (34 percent) compared to all filers (38 percent).

The application of our two business tests eliminates 1.1 million Schedule F filers from our business group. Nearly all of those filers failed our first *de minimis* business test. The filers we exclude reported an average of $2,900 of total income and -$200 of net income.

Form 1065: Partnerships
For partnerships, we make two modifications to our business tests. We exclude any ordinary income received from another partnership, estate or trust (line 4, Form 1065) to eliminate double counting of income. As noted in the previous section, we also exclude any guaranteed payments to partners from our analysis. Both the deductions (line 10) and income amounts (Schedule K, line 4) reflect a return to partners for services provided and so are similar to distributions that partners receive.

For partnership and S corporation tests and tabulations, we include all investment income and deductions reported separately on the Schedule K (except for guaranteed payments to partners).[18] We also include gross rents and any deductions reported on Form 8825 (Rental Real Estate Income and Expenses of a Partnership or S Corporation). Partnerships and S corporations report rental income and associated deductions on Form 8825. The resultant net income is then transferred to Schedule K.

For tax year 2007, 3.1 million partnerships filed Form 1065. Those partnerships reported gross receipts of $3.9 trillion, gross rents of $424 billion (Form 8825), investment income of $1.8 trillion (Schedule K), and net income of $1.5 trillion (includes ordinary and investment income, average profit of

---

[18] Partnerships and S corporations report investment (i.e., capital gains, dividends, and interest), royalty and rental income on Schedule K and not on the front page of the main form (Form 1065 or Form 1120S). Those amounts are reported separately because the apportionment rules for the owners may differ compared to the apportionment of ordinary business income. Income reported on the Schedule K retains its character when passed through to the partner or shareholder, and so might face different tax rates or limitations than distributions of ordinary business income. Deductions reported on the Schedule K include investment interest expense, the Section 179 expensing deduction and miscellaneous "other" deductions.

$488,300). The 2.3 million partnerships (74 percent of total) we deem a business reported gross receipts of $3.9 trillion, gross rents of $417 billion, investment income of $1.7 trillion and net income of $1.4 trillion (average profit of $615,300). The proportion of partnerships that were profitable is higher for our business group (61 percent) compared to all partnerships (57 percent).

The application of our two business tests eliminates 0.8 million partnerships from our business group. Of the partnerships we exclude: 0.6 million failed our first *de minimis* business test, 0.1 million were deemed an investment vehicle and 0.1 million reported insufficient deductions. The partnerships we exclude reported an average of $155,700 of total income and $121,800 of net income.

Form 1120S: S Corporations
For tax year 2007, 4.0 million S corporations filed Form 1120S. Those corporations reported gross receipts of $6.0 trillion, gross rents of $39 billion (Form 8825), investment income of $290 billion (Schedule K), and net income of $424 billion (includes ordinary and investment income, average profit of $106,400). The 3.6 million corporations (89 percent of total) we deem a business reported gross receipts of $6.0 trillion, gross rents of $38 billion, investment income of $284 billion and net income of $419 billion (average profit of $117,900). The proportion of corporations that were profitable is higher for our business group (68 percent) compared to all corporations (64 percent).

The application of our two business tests eliminates 0.4 million S corporations from our business group. Most of the corporations we exclude failed our first *de minimis* business test. The corporations we exclude reported an average of $17,700 of total income and $12,200 of net income.

Form 1120: C Corporations
For tax year 2007, 1.9 million C corporations filed Form 1120. Those corporations reported gross receipts of $18.2 trillion, gross rents of $102 billion, investment income of $3.7 trillion (mostly interest) and net income of $1.1 trillion (average profit of $568,700). The 1.6 million corporations (88 percent of total) we deem a business reported gross receipts of $18.2 trillion, gross rents of $102 billion, investment income of $3.7 trillion and net income of $1.1 trillion (average profit of $646,100). The proportion of corporations that were profitable is higher for our business group (54 percent) compared to all corporations (51 percent).

The application of our two business tests eliminates 0.2 million C corporations from our business group. Most of the corporations we exclude failed our first *de minimis* business test. The corporations we exclude reported an average of $24,500 of total income and $10,600 of net income.

At the bottom of Table 1, we show totals for all filers that qualify as a business based on the two tests we apply. We retain more than one half (55 percent) of all entities that file a business return. Those entities reported nearly all total income and net income of the full population of filers. On average, the entities we exclude reported $13,500 of total income and $8,200 of net income.

Sensitivity to Business Tests
In Table 3, we adjust the thresholds used for our two business tests to examine the sensitivity of our thresholds (labeled as Test 3). If we reduce our *de minimis* income and deduction threshold to $5,000 and reduce the deduction floor to $1,000 (Test 1), this does increase the number of business entities, but the additional entities are generally quite small. The greatest impact is for Schedule C filers. Using Test

1 thresholds, the number of Schedule C filers increases by 3.2 million relative to the thresholds we employ (Test 3). Those 3.2 million filers reported average total income of $11,200 and average net income of $5,400. Based on these results, our thresholds appear to serve their intended purpose: the elimination of small entities that are less likely to be engaged in businesslike activity, if at all.

III.   Identification of Small Businesses

In the previous section, we applied two tests to separate filers into business and non-business groups. Those tests represent one possible method to distinguish businesses from other taxpayers, and we recognize that any such attempt must rely on subjective criteria. Similarly, there is no single definition or unique set of characteristics that should always be used to distinguish small businesses from their larger counterparts; an appropriate definition in one context might be inappropriate for other purposes. The tax code reflects this ambiguity because it contains no explicit definition of small business. Rather, various code sections grant favorable tax treatment to certain filers based on their level of investment, taxable income, or gross receipts. Some examples are as follows[19]:

- Expensing of Investment. Under IRC Section 179, for qualified investment placed in service during tax year 2007 (the year from which our data are drawn), eligible firms could expense up to $125,000 of qualified investment (generally machinery, equipment and software); if firms had qualifying investment that exceeded $500,000, then the expensing deduction was phased-out dollar-for-dollar for investment above that limit. For 2008 and 2009, the limits were raised to $250,000 (expensing) and $800,000 (beginning of phase out); for 2010 and 2011, the limits were raised to $500,000 and $2 million, respectively. For 2012, the expensing limits decline to $125,000 and $500,000 (indexed for inflation from 2006). For 2013, the limits revert to $25,000 and $200,000.[20]

- Graduated Corporate Rates. C corporations face a graduated rate schedule based on their reported taxable income: 15 percent (taxable income less than $50,000), 25 percent ($50,000 to $75,000), 34 percent ($75,000 to $18.3 million, but certain income faces surcharges within that range to eliminate the benefit of lower rates) and 35 percent (greater than $18.3 million).

- Business Start-Up Costs. Under IRC Section 195, a business can elect to deduct up to $5,000 ($10,000 for 2010) of start-up expenditures in the taxable year in which the active trade or business begins. The $5,000/$10,000 amount is reduced dollar-for-dollar by the amount that cumulative start-up expenditures exceed $50,000 ($60,000 for 2010). Start-up expenditures that are not deductible in the year the active trade or business begins are, at the taxpayer's election, amortized over a 15-year period. Otherwise, taxpayers must capitalize those expenses.

- Cash Method Accounting. Under IRC Section 446, firms must use the same method of accounting for financial and tax purposes. In general, firms that maintain inventories must use the accrual method to compute taxable income. Section 448 prohibits corporations and partnerships with corporate partners from using cash method accounting. However, an exception

---

[19] For descriptions of these and other tax code provisions that provide favorable tax treatment to businesses based on size, see Gary Guenther, "Small Business Tax Benefits: Overview of Current Law and Economic Justification," CRS Report, April 19, 2010.

[20] These limits reflect changes enacted by various acts, including The Small Business and Work Opportunity Tax Act of 2007, The Economic Stimulus Act of 2008, The American Recovery and Reinvestment Act of 2009, The Small Business Jobs Act of 2010, and The Tax Relief and Unemployment Insurance Reauthorization and Job Creation Act of 2010.

is made if average annual gross receipts from the prior three years is less than $5 million. IRS Revenue Procedure 2002-28 extends cash method accounting to firms in "non-inventory intensive" industries if they have average annual gross receipts that are less than $10 million.

- Simplified Dollar-Value LIFO. Businesses that maintain inventories generally use "first-in-first-out" (FIFO) or "last-in-first-out" (LIFO) inventory valuation methods. Under IRC Section 474, firms with average annual gross receipts of $5 million or less in the previous three years may use a simplified version dollar-value LIFO.

Because many tax code provisions use gross receipts to identify firms eligible for preferential treatment and because filers do not report the number of employees on their tax returns, we use a total income threshold to separate small businesses from their larger counterparts. We define total income as the sum of gross receipts, rents and any portfolio income reported by the firm.[21] We set the small business threshold at $10 million of total income. Because deductions can reflect the scale of operations, we also require that total deductions not exceed $10 million.[22]

Table 4 presents results from the application of the $10 million total income and deduction threshold to all entities deemed a business in Table 1. The vast majority of entities deemed a business also qualify as a small business. However, small businesses reported less than one-fifth of gross receipts, approximately two-thirds of gross rental income, less than one-tenth of gross investment income and less than one-fifth of net income reported by all business entities. Not unexpectedly, small businesses reported a larger share of business losses (48 percent) than profits (23 percent).

Tables 5 through 8 present small business tabulations based on total income, net income, industry, and employer/non-employer status. As shown by Table 5, slightly more than one-half of small businesses reported less than $50,000 of total income each; half of those businesses reported a tax loss for the year (not shown in table). At the other end of the spectrum, approximately 1.4 million small businesses (6 percent) reported more than $1 million of total income each. Only one-quarter of these larger firms reported a tax loss for the year.

Table 6 presents small business tabulations based on net income. Approximately two-fifths of all small businesses reported a tax loss; another one-half reported a profit less than $50,000. For those businesses, gross receipts comprised the vast majority of their reported income. By comparison, only 0.5 percent of small businesses reported a profit in excess of $1 million. For those businesses, investment and rental income comprised roughly half of their reported income.

Table 7 presents small business tabulations based on industry. One-half of small businesses are in the construction, real estate-rental or professional-technical sectors. Businesses in those sectors reported nearly two-fifths of total income and one-half of net income. Only the agriculture sector reported a tax loss, which was caused by Form 1040 Schedule F filers.

---

[21] For these purposes, we include "other income" reported by the firm on the front page of the tax form or schedule. We continue to use absolute values for income fields that can be negative, such as sales of business assets.

[22] If we double the small business threshold from $10 to $20 million, then we add approximately 110,000 entities that report average total income of $13.2 million and average net income of $1.1 million.

In Table 8, we separate small businesses into employer and non-employer groups. We classify a business as an "employer" if labor deductions exceed $10,000.[23] For corporations, we continue to exclude payments to officers from labor expenses. For sole proprietors, we include expenses for "contract labor" (line 11, Schedule C) because much of those expenses relate to the employment of independent contractors who are similar to employees of the business.[24] (Other business filers do not separately itemize expenses for contract labor.) To the extent that payments for contract labor are also reported as gross receipts on a business tax return by the recipients and the recipients are included in our small business group and counted as an employer, then the number of employers will be overstated. Finally, we count all Schedule E Rental Real Estate Income filers as non-employers, although it is possible that a small proportion have labor expenses in excess of our $10,000 threshold.[25]

Based on these criteria, we find that slightly more than one-fifth of small businesses qualify as an employer. Employers were considerably larger than non-employers, reporting average total income of $922,100, compared to $99,900 for non-employers, and average net income of $45,300, compared to $15,500 for non-employers.

Table 9 presents small business tabulations for wage and depreciation deductions based on total income. Approximately three-fifths of corporations, one-quarter of partnerships and one-fifth of sole proprietors (excludes payments to contract labor) made any wage payment to labor employed directly by the firm. Total wages paid were $945 billion, an average of $174,200 per small business that reported any wage expense. Relative to all business entities regardless of size, small businesses reported 23 percent of total labor payments made to employees who were not owners/officers of the firm (not shown in table).

Small corporations also made substantial wage payments to owners/officers of the firm ($278 billion) who should receive "reasonable compensation" for any services they provide.[26] For the purposes of this analysis, we have not included those wage payments in our definition of net business income. Rather, we define business income as the residual income that accrues to owners after all expenses have been paid, including any wage payments to owners. For small corporate business owners, the distinction between returns to labor (wages or compensation of officers) and returns to capital (distributions or dividends) is somewhat arbitrary and will vary with the type of business entity.[27] For example, C corporation owners have a greater incentive to pay themselves higher levels of reasonable wage compensation in order to avoid the double tax levied on corporate profits and dividend distributions. By contrast, S corporation owners likely minimize their overall tax liability by maximizing distributions from the corporation, thereby avoiding payroll taxes.[28] Future analysis might explore the implications of

---

[23] For this purpose, we include deductions for wages-salaries reported on the front page of business returns, cost of labor (Schedule A, Cost of Goods Sold) and any wages-salaries reported by partnerships and S corporations on Form 8825.

[24] Per the Schedule C instructions: "Contract labor includes payments to persons you do not treat as employees (for example, independent contractors) for services performed for your trade or business. Do not include contract labor deducted elsewhere on your return, such as contract labor that is includible on line 17 (legal and professional services), 21 (repairs and maintenance), 26 (wages) or 37 (cost of labor, Schedule A)."

[25] For Schedule E filers, we do not have the information necessary to make this computation.

[26] The data do not perfectly distinguish between owners and non-owners. Some owners may receive payments classified as wages, while officers who are not owners may receive officer compensation.

[27] For a more complete discussion of this issue, see Bull and Burnham, "Taxation of Capital and Labor: The Diverse Landscape by Entity Type," National Tax Journal, September 2010, p. 397-412.

[28] These different incentives appear to be borne out by tax data. Small S corporations report a much higher profit margin on sales compared to their C corporation counterparts, and most of the difference can be explained by payments for labor services, especially for officers/owners. This result holds generally even when we control for firm size and industry.

a more expansive definition of business income that includes wage compensation paid to corporate owners.

The final columns of Table 9 show depreciation deductions reported by small businesses. Across all entities, depreciation deductions totaled $142 billion, an average of $15,100 per firm for firms that report a depreciation deduction. That total includes $47 billion of Section 179 expensing deductions, comprising nearly one-third of total depreciation deductions. Relative to all business entities regardless of size, small businesses reported 19 percent of total depreciation deductions (not shown in table). It is likely that the small business share of total investment is roughly similar.

IV.   Identifying Small Business Owners

Having identified entities that meet our small business and employer criteria, the final step in our methodology is identifying the individuals who own those businesses. To do this, we link individual taxpayers to the businesses they own. This task is straightforward for Form 1040 Schedule C, E (rentals) and F filers because those schedules are filed with the individual's income tax return. It is more complicated for individuals who report partnership and/or S corporation income because we must link the Form 1040 individual income tax return to the business return of the entities they own to ensure that the income is attributable to a small business. This linkage is made possible with newly accessible data from IRS's Compliance Data Warehouse (CDW). The CDW stores unedited data from all tax returns – business, individual, and information – filed with the IRS. In the sections below, we first describe how we match partners and S corporation shareholders to the small business entities they own. Those matches are then combined with the data from Schedules C, E rental and F to show distributions of small business income and their owners by AGI and marginal tax rate groupings.[29]

Note on Owners of Small C Corporations

In the tables from the previous section, we included C corporations in all small business tabulations. Using data from the CDW, it would be possible to link individuals to some of the C corporations they own by tracing dividends paid by those firms through to the individual income tax returns of their owners. However, the receipt of dividends is the only indicator of C corporation ownership in the data. In practice, many individuals do not receive dividends from the C corporations they own, making dividends a poor indicator of C corporation ownership. Many C corporations are unable to pay dividends because they report losses, which cannot be passed through to owners. Unlike S corporations, C corporations need not allocate for tax purposes all earnings to their owners. Tax data show that only a portion of their after-tax earnings are paid out to owners as dividends. Rather than pay dividends, owners might retain after-tax profits in the corporation and smooth their taxable income by distributing retained earnings when funds are needed most, such as when the business suffers a loss.[30] In this manner, owners could minimize tax liability by making distributions during years they face lower

---

[29] Bull, Nelson, and Fisher, "Characteristics of Business Ownership: Overview for Passthrough Entities and Evidence on S Corporate Ownership from Linked Data," forthcoming National Tax Journal, used similar IRS data linking S corporations to the individual Form 1040 and estate and trust Form 1041 tax returns of their owners. B-N-F started with the entity return and then found the return of the owner, whereas in this paper we start with the return of the individual and find the partnership and S corporation returns owned by those individuals.

[30] For example, small C corporations reporting a tax loss distributed more than $1.5 billion in cash distributions to owners in 2007.

marginal tax rates. Owners might also retain earnings to finance future capital outlays. Finally, if owners elect to distribute earnings to themselves as wage compensation rather than dividends, then the data generally do not allow us to readily distinguish employees who are owners from those who are not. For these reasons, the receipt of dividends is an imperfect indicator of C corporation ownership, and owners who report dividend distributions in any given year will not be representative of all C corporation owners. We therefore exclude small C corporation owners from the tabulations presented in this section.

Identification of Small Business Partners and S Corporation Shareholders

Individuals report their income or loss from partnerships and S corporations on Part II of Form 1040, Schedule E. Specifically, for each partnership or S corporation, they report the entity's Employer Identification Number (EIN), the amount of ordinary business income or loss (including any net rental income), and whether the income is passive or active. They also report any Section 179 expense deductions that flowed through from their partnership or S corporation interests. We start with a list of Schedule E EINs prepared by SOI for the 2007 Individual Sole Proprietorship (INSOLE) tax file.[31] For the 126,344 (unweighted) individuals who reported partnership or S corporation income on the 2007 INSOLE file, SOI recorded 1.14 million total EINs, an average of nine EINs per individual.[32] (See Table 10, column 1.) Because many individuals were partners or shareholders in multiple entities, there were 526,511 distinct EINs; 377,609 reported as partnerships, 146,271 reported S corporations, and 2,631 reported sometimes as partnerships, sometimes as S corporations.[33] We looked for the Partnership Form 1065 and S Corporation Form 1120S returns associated with these 526,511 unique EINs on the CDW and found 93 percent of the partnership EINs and 96 percent of the S corporation EINs. (Table 10, column 3.) We use these matches to identify the owners of entities that meet our small business definition.

Table 11 presents additional detail on the success of matching EINs reported on INSOLE to CDW entities. It shows the returns and income for partnership and S corporation gains and losses, according to whether the individual reported it as active or passive income. Unlike Table 10, these data are weighted to yield population totals.[34] Overall, the EINs found on the CDW reflect 94 percent of partnership and 97 percent of S corporation net income or loss reported on the INSOLE Schedule E. Ninety-two percent of individuals reporting partnership income or loss, and 94 percent of those reporting S corporation income or loss have at least one of their partnership or S corporation EINs found on the CDW.

---

[31] INSOLE is the primary file of individual income tax returns that SOI prepares annually and that the Treasury Department uses for tax analysis. The file is a nationally representative, stratified random sample of individual income tax returns filed during calendar year 2008. For more information on the sample, see "Description of the Sample," Statistics of Income 2007, Individual Income Tax Returns, IRS 2009.

[32] This unweighted average is high because high-income taxpayers, who typically have more holdings, are disproportionately represented in this unweighted data set.

[33] These could reflect taxpayer error or they could be explained by partners or shareholders not being aware that entities had changed their form of organization. In particular, limited liability companies, which usually file partnership returns, can "check the box" to be treated as a corporation and then elect to be treated as an S corporation.

[34] In general, we were somewhat more successful in finding the entity tax returns of (1) S corporation shareholders than partners, and (2) gains versus losses. With passive losses, this outcome might be attributable to reported losses that were previously disallowed from entities that no longer exist.

For the entity returns of the 493,993 EINs found on the CDW (Table 10), we applied our "business," "small business," and "employer" criteria described in Part II of this paper.[35] Table 12 displays the (weighted) results from applying these criteria at the entity level and then following those designations through to business owners who file individual income tax returns.[36] Overall, 99 percent of partnership and S corporation net income reported on Schedule E comes from firms meeting our "business" definition, and 49 percent comes from "small businesses." (See column 2.) For partners, 84 percent of returns reporting 101 percent of net income are deemed a business entity based on our tests. (Columns 4 and 5.) Application of our small business thresholds reduces those figures to 71 percent and 46 percent, respectively. For S corporation shareholders, 89 percent of returns and 98 percent of net income were attributable to a business entity, while 85 percent of returns and 52 percent of net income were attributable to small businesses.[37]

Table 12 also highlights the partners and shareholders of entities that meet our business test, but are not small (generally gross receipts in excess of $10 million). Thirteen percent of partners and S corporation shareholders own businesses that are not small, but the net income they receive from those businesses represents half of all net partnership and S corporation income reported by individuals. (Individuals may own both small and not small businesses.[38]) The tabulations show that a larger share of partners (18 percent) than S corporation shareholders (6 percent) own firms that are not small, and a somewhat larger share of partnership net income (55 percent) than S corporation net income (46 percent) comes from these larger businesses. However, the average net income for owners of larger S corporations is nearly $500,000, compared to $114,000 for partners in the larger partnerships.

The bottom of Table 12 shows results from applying our employer business definition to partnerships and S corporations. As shown, many more S corporation shareholders than partners own businesses that are employers – 2.0 million vs. 958,000 – representing 49 percent of S corporation shareholders, but only 23 percent of partners. For both forms of business, most income (76 and 79 percent) is attributable to employer firms. Although most employers are also small businesses (2.4 million, or 85 percent), small business employers account for less than half of the net income reported by employer firms ($132 billion, or 40 percent) and are roughly half as large based on average net income.

---

[35] Because CDW data lack certain detail, we approximate the definitions using the variables available. The main gaps in the CDW data are (1) the absence of expense itemization from Form 8825 (Rental Real Estate Income and Expenses, only total available), (2) lack of separate itemization of labor costs embedded in cost of goods sold, (3) investment interest expense from the Schedule K, (4) certain Schedule D detail (Capital Gains and Losses, only net amounts are available), and (5) certain Form 4797 detail (Sales of Business Property, only net amounts are available). Because these fields are generally minimal for small businesses, this lack of detail has minor implications for our results.

[36] The income figures reported on individual income tax returns differ from amounts reported by the entities and discussed in the earlier section of this paper for several reasons besides missing returns. Most importantly, for both partnerships and S corporations, the data here are only what is reported on Schedule E, ordinary trade or business and rental income. It does not include capital gains, interest, dividends and other portfolio income. In addition, not all owners are individuals, which is particularly true for partnerships.

[37] The total number of returns exceeds the sum of the number of partners and S corporation shareholders in Table 11 because many taxpayers are both partners and S corporation shareholders. Indeed, while most partners or shareholders (70 percent) report only one EIN of either type on their Schedule E, 13 percent report both S corporation and partnership income or loss. Taxpayers with only one EIN account for 40 percent of partnership and S corporation net income; those with both an S corporation and a partnership EIN account for another 37 percent of net income.

[38] Individuals may appear in both categories but business income appears only once, in its appropriate size category.

17

Table 13 details the types of income that partners and S corporation shareholders receive (active or passive, gain or loss) from businesses, small businesses, and employer businesses. Table 13 shows that roughly the same number of partners receive active income as passive income from their businesses (1.4 million each – column 1), but that S corporation shareholders are seldom passive (2.4 million vs. 394,000 – column 5). Similarly for losses: nearly as many partners receive passive losses from businesses (848,000 – column 3) as active losses (912,000) but over 10 times as many S corporation shareholders (1.2 million – column 7) receive active losses as passive (100,000). Active income and loss also far exceed passive income and loss for both partnership and S corporation owners.[39]

Compared to active or passive partners or passive shareholders, active S corporation shareholders account for a larger portion of small business income ($168 billion) and small business owners (2.2 million). Almost all - 91 percent - of active S corporation shareholders own small businesses, compared to 69 percent of active partners. Fifty-seven percent of active S corporation income comes from small businesses, versus only 44 percent for partnerships. Conversely, partners report a larger share of passive income from small businesses compared to S corporation shareholders.

Table 13 also shows owners of employer businesses according to whether they are active or passive partners or S corporation shareholders. The data show that active S corporation shareholders of small business employers reported nearly two-fifths ($114 billion) of total positive active S corporation income. By contrast, active partners of small business employers reported only one quarter ($47 billion) of total positive active partnership income. The data also confirm that few passive partners or S corporation shareholders own employer firms, small or otherwise.

All Flow-through Entities

Having identified the owners of small business partnerships and S corporations, we then combine those results with small business income attributable to sole proprietorships, farming and rental real estate activities. However, merely identifying individuals who report income from a small business is insufficient to deem the individual a "small business owner." We must also consider other characteristics of the owner. Relevant characteristics include:

- Owners of Large and Small Businesses. If filers own multiple businesses, some small and some not small, when should they be considered small business owners: if they own any small business, regardless of other ownership, or only if their small business income bears some specific relationship to their large business income? What if they own multiple small businesses that, if added together, would not be small?
- Active vs. Passive Income. Should owners with passive interests be deemed small business owners, or only those who actively participate in the business? Passive investors often provide the capital that makes a business possible; changes in tax policy that affect the after-tax return on their investments might influence their willingness to invest. However, popular discussions of small business owners often focus on active owners who make the operating decisions.
- Significance Relative to Adjusted Gross Income (AGI). Should income from the small business be "material" to the owner for the filer to be considered a "small business owner"? Or does any amount of small business income make someone a "small business owner"?

---

[39] The sum of the number of returns in Table 12 exceeds the totals in Table 11 because taxpayers can report both active and passive, and gain and loss attributable to multiple entities.

Because there are no obvious answers to these questions, we use two possible definitions of small business owner. Under our "broad" definition, we include anyone who reports income or loss from an entity that meets our definition of small business. Under our "narrow" definition, we only include individuals whose active income or loss from small business represents at least 25 percent of their AGI; all passive income and losses are disregarded. Under both definitions, small business owners may also own large or even very large businesses.

Results for Small Business Owners

Tables 14 through 16 present our results by AGI class while Tables 17 and 18 use statutory marginal tax rates. Table 14 compares distributions of tax returns across six groups: all returns; returns with any flow-through net income; all business owners; small business owners under our broad and narrow definitions; and business owners with income or loss from businesses too big to be considered small under our definition. (Note that business owners in the last group – those with businesses too big to be considered small – may also own small businesses and be counted as small business owners.) For tax year 2007, three percent of all returns and 33 percent of AGI were reported by taxpayers with AGI over $200,000 (mean AGI of $625,000, median of $300,000). For taxpayers reporting any flow-through income, eight percent of taxpayers reporting 75 percent of net flow-through income reported AGI over $200,000 (mean AGI of $760,000, median of $325,000). If we restrict our focus to small business owners (broad definition), then 11 percent of returns reporting 64 percent of small business income reported AGI over $200,000 (mean AGI of $800,000, median of $335,000). Using the narrow definition of small business owner, eight percent of returns and 57 percent of narrowly defined small business income were reported by taxpayers in the upper income classes (mean AGI of $480,000, median of $315,000). Taxpayers owning any business too big to meet the broad definition of small business -- here called "owners of any larger business" – are more concentrated in the upper income groups (49 percent reported AGI over $200,000, with mean AGI of $1.7 million and median over $500,000) and reported more than 100 percent of the net income from larger businesses (because of net losses and small amounts of positive income reported by lower AGI classes).

Table 15 compares recipients of any flow-through income to employer owners – owners of businesses that meet our definition of employer or small business employer (under the broad definition of small business owner). Of the 34.7 million taxpayers with flow-through income, 4.3 million own a business that is an employer, and 3.8 million of those taxpayers own small businesses. Overall, owners of small business employers and the income from those businesses are more concentrated in the upper income ranges than is true for small businesses in general. (Compare with Table 14.)

Table 16 presents the sources of income by AGI class for small business owners under three definitions: broad, narrow, and small business employer. The right-hand columns show other sources of income for small business owners, such as wages and capital gains. The table highlights the importance of wages and other forms of income for all three sets of small business owners.[40] This is less true under the narrow definition of small business owner because small business income must comprise at least 25 percent of AGI for those taxpayers.

---

[40] Wages and salaries could include officer compensation for S corporation owners.

Tables 17 and 18 present statutory marginal tax rates faced by small business owners. They show the distribution of returns and net income for various types of taxpayers and small business owners with positive taxable income by their statutory marginal tax rate.[41] [42] We note that the tabulations in Tables 17 and 18 include all business losses passed through to taxpayers, as long as taxable income remains positive. It is appropriate to include both positive and negative sources of income – as long as the taxpayer reports positive taxable income -- because the tax value of losses varies with the taxpayer's marginal tax rate. Tables 17 and 18 also separately break out taxpayers who have AMT liability and face marginal rates of 26 percent or 28 percent.

Table 17 shows that one percent of all taxpayers with positive taxable income faced the 33- or 35-percent marginal rate for tax year 2007. That share increases to three or four percent for taxpayers with any flow-through income and owners of small businesses (broad and narrow definitions). The share rises to 20 percent for owners of non-small businesses. In terms of income, a smaller share of net small business income went to taxpayers in the top brackets – 32 and 29 percent under the broad and narrow definitions, respectively – compared to 50 percent of all flow-through income. For owners of larger businesses, 86 percent of net income from those businesses went to taxpayers in the top two rate brackets.[43]

Table 18 shows similar distributions for owners of employer businesses. Owners of employer businesses are more concentrated in the top rate brackets than are recipients of flow-through income in general: 12 percent for all employers and 10 percent for small business employers, compared to three percent for all taxpayers with flow-through income. A larger share of net income from employer businesses goes to top-bracket taxpayers – 61 percent – than to either small business employers – 38 percent – or taxpayers with flow-through income in general – 50 percent.

Comparison with Other Analyses

To the extent that our analysis is similar to methodologies used by other studies, we find that the results are generally comparable. Specifically, the Joint Committee on Taxation (JCT) and the Urban-Brookings Tax Policy Center (TPC) have published estimates of taxpayers with any flow-through income who would fall into the 36 or 39.6 percent rate brackets in 2011 under the Administration's FY11 Budget proposal to let the tax cuts expire for taxpayers with income over $200,000 (single returns) or $250,000 (joint returns):

---

[41] The statutory marginal tax rate is the rate applicable to the last dollar of taxable income. That rate may or may not equal the "effective marginal tax rate" depending on certain phase-outs and credits. The effective marginal tax rate is equal to the change in tax liability associated with the last dollar of taxable income, divided by 100. The approach used by this technical paper is similar to that used by IRS' Statistics of Income Division in their various individual income tax publications.

[42] Tables 17 and 18 exclude filers who fail to report any positive taxable income (i.e., a zero percent statutory tax rate). For small business owners, zero taxable income could result from business losses that cannot be used to offset taxable income. Inclusion of those filers would effectively double count the impact of unused business losses for small business owners because our tabulations also reflect unused business losses carried forward from prior years that are used to offset current year taxable income. For all filers, this omission excludes 32.3 million filers reporting $198 billion of AGI. For our broad (narrow) definition of small business owner, 4.9 million (3.6 million) owners are excluded who reported -$37 billion (-$21 billion) of small business income.

[43] For tax year 2007, the mean and median AGI for taxpayers in the top two tax brackets was $1.2 million and $500,000, respectively. For small business owners who faced the 33 or 35 percent tax rates, the mean and median AGI were $1.4 million and $600,000 (broad definition) or $750,000 and $475,000 (narrow definition). Top bracket taxpayers owning any larger businesses had mean AGI of $2.8 million and mean of $1.1 million.

- The staff of the Joint Committee on Taxation estimates that in 2011 just under 750,000 taxpayers with net positive business income (3 percent of all taxpayers with net positive business income) will have marginal rates of 36 or 39.6 percent under the President's proposal, and that 50 percent of the approximately $1 trillion of aggregate net positive business income will be reported on returns that have a marginal rate of 36 or 39.6 percent. [44]

- The Tax Policy Center estimates that 3.2 percent of tax units reporting net positive business income would be affected by the "Administration's upper-income tax proposals," and those taxpayers would report 44 percent of positive business income (net negative business income is not included). [45]

Although the precise number of taxpayers with flow-through income (business income to the JCT or TPC) and the dollar amount of that income in the top rate brackets varies among the three analyses, the conclusions are broadly consistent: about three percent of taxpayers with flow-through income fall into the top rate brackets, either in 2007 or under proposed 2011 law, and they report a substantial share of all flow-through income (45 – 50 percent).

Our analysis goes a step further and separates taxpayers who receive flow-through income into small business owners and others. We find that using flow-through income as a proxy for "small business owner" slightly understates the share of owners in the top rate brackets (4.3 percent of small business owners vs. 3.2 percent of all flow-through recipients) but considerably overstates the share of small business income under our broad definition (32 percent vs. 50 percent). Our analysis can also identify taxpayers who own employer and small employer businesses. We find that 14 percent of taxpayers reporting flow-through income or loss and positive taxable income own at least one business that meets our definition of "employer." However, that figure increases to 51 percent for individuals in the two top rate brackets. [46] For small business employers, the comparable figures are 12 and 37 percent.

V. Conclusion

This technical paper presents a revised methodology to improve the identification of small businesses and their owners for the purpose of tax policy analysis. In the first section, we identify small businesses. We apply two tests to separate business from non-business entities. We then further sub-divide filers we identify as business entities into small and other businesses based on a $10 million gross income and deduction test. Overall, approximately 54 percent of filers across the six tax forms and schedules we consider meet the criteria we use to define a small business. Those entities reported 18 percent of total business income (average of $270,000) and 16 percent of net business income (average of $21,600) for tax year 2007. Approximately half of our small businesses reported total income less than $50,000, and almost 90 percent reported net income less than $50,000. Roughly half are in the real estate-rental,

---

[44] Joint Committee on Taxation, Description of Revenue Provisions Contained in the President's Fiscal Year 2011 Budget Proposal. JCS-2-10, August 16, 2010, p. 25. The measure of business income is the same as our measure of individual's flow-through income, except that the JCT includes royalties, trusts and estates, and real estate mortgage investment conduits.

[45] TPC includes non-filers and returns with zero taxable income in its base. Business income is defined as those who report an income or loss on Schedules C, E or F. Source: *http://taxpolicycenter.org/numbers/Content/Excel/T10-0186.xls*.

[46] Calculations based on Table 18: column 5 divided by column 1.

construction or professional-scientific sectors. Based on our definition of employer (direct labor compensation exceeds $10,000), we find that slightly more than one-fifth of small businesses were also employers.

In the second section, we apply our small business criteria to newly accessible tax data to link income reported by small businesses to their respective owner(s). We present results for two definitions of small business owner. Under our broad definition, we include any individual who reports flow-through income from a small business regardless of the relative significance of that income to the owner or its nature (active or passive). Under our narrow definition, we only count individuals as small business owners if their active net small business income comprises at least one quarter of their AGI.

Due to data constraints, our prior methodology counted all taxpayers reporting flow-through income as small business owners. Using that approach, there are 34.7 million small business owners reporting $662 billion of net business income (average of $19,100) for tax year 2007. (See Table 14.) Eight percent of those filers (with three-quarters of the net business income) reported AGI over $200,000. Using our revised methodology and our broad definition of small business owner, we identify 20.0 million small business owners reporting $376 billion of net small business income (average of $18,800). Eleven percent of those filers (with nearly two-thirds of net small business income) reported AGI over $200,000. Using our narrow definition of small business owner, we identify 9.4 million filers reporting $335 billion of net small business income (average of $35,600) as small business owners. Eight percent of those filers (with 57 percent of net small business income) reported AGI over $200,000. Finally, we identify 1.2 million filers who owned businesses too large to be considered small; they reported $205 billion in net income from those businesses. (Many of those filers also own small businesses and are counted as small business owners using either our broad or narrow definition of owner.)

In Table 17, we present tabulations based on the statutory marginal tax rate faced by filers we identify as small business owners. For those purposes, we only consider filers who report positive taxable income (but might report business losses). For tax year 2007, approximately one percent of all filers reporting sixteen percent of total AGI faced one of the two top statutory tax rates. If we only consider individuals who report any flow-through income, then three percent of filers reporting half of flow-through net income faced the top two tax rates. Using our broad definition of small business owner, four percent of filers reporting one-third of small business net income faced the top two tax rates. Using our narrow definition, those figures are four and 29 percent respectively. Our revised methodology reduces the relative share of small business income subject to the highest tax rate brackets because it excludes income passed through from business entities that reported income or deductions in excess of $10 million. Table 17 also shows that 20 percent of taxpayers owning any larger businesses, and $190 billion of net income, fall into the top two tax rate brackets.

Although our methodology is but one approach that could be used to more accurately identify small business owners, we find that our basic conclusions are not sensitive to the tests we apply. Our analysis highlights the need for policymakers to more explicitly define the characteristics that distinguish a small business so that the impact of targeted tax provisions can be modeled appropriately.

Table 1: Business Versus Non-Business Filers
tax year 2007, billions of dollars, thousands of filers

	Number of Filers	Total Income Detail					Net Income Detail			
		Gross Receipts	Gross Rents 1/	Other Income 2/	Total Income	Avg Total Income	Pos Net Income	Neg Net Income	Net Income	Avg Net Income
Schedule C: Sole Proprietors										
All Filers	23,175	1,351	na	20	1,371	59,177	335	-55	280	12,069
Business	10,684	1,266	na	18	1,284	120,209	268	-45	223	20,854
Non-Business	12,491	85	na	2	87	6,974	66	-10	57	4,555
Schedule E: Rent										
All Filers	9,636	na	255	na	255	26,456	57	-74	-18	-1,825
Business	4,593	na	212	na	212	46,238	38	-60	-22	-4,755
Non-Business	5,043	na	43	na	43	8,442	18	-14	4	844
Schedule F: Farmers										
All Filers	2,511	107	na	26	134	53,254	14	-27	-13	-5,295
Business	1,415	106	na	25	130	92,194	12	-25	-13	-9,208
Non-Business	1,095	2	na	1	3	2,940	2	-2	0	-239
Form 1065: Partnerships										
All Filers	3,096	3,900	424	1,848	6,172	1,993,325	1,857	-345	1,512	488,319
Business	2,300	3,838	417	1,743	6,048	2,629,841	1,732	-317	1,415	615,282
Non-Business	797	12	7	105	124	155,666	125	-28	97	121,771
Form 1120-S: S Corporations										
All Filers	3,990	5,974	39	290	6,302	1,579,574	509	-84	424	106,369
Business	3,554	5,973	38	284	6,295	1,770,991	501	-82	419	117,914
Non-Business	436	2	0	6	8	17,745	8	-2	5	12,167
Form 1120: C Corporations										
All Filers	1,865	18,243	102	3,666	22,011	11,800,554	1,308	-247	1,061	568,723
Business	1,638	18,242	102	3,661	22,005	13,433,466	1,305	-247	1,058	646,119
Non-Business	227	1	0	4	6	24,478	3	-1	2	10,566
TOTAL										
All Filers	44,273	29,576	819	5,850	36,245	818,678	4,079	-833	3,246	73,319
Business	24,184	29,474	769	5,731	35,975	1,487,559	3,857	-776	3,080	127,375
Non-Business	20,089	102	50	118	270	13,450	222	-56	166	8,243

1/ For partnerships and S corporations, includes any gross rents reported on Form 8825.

2/ For partnerships and S corporations, includes all income reported on Schedule K, except net rental real estate income.
For partnerships and all corporations, includes net capital gains, dividends, royalties, interest and miscellaneous other income.

Table 2: Non-Business Sole Proprietorships
tax year 2007, billions of dollars, thousands of filers

Total Income, Sch C		Net Income, Schedule C			Net Income, Schedule E			Wages-Salaries			Adjusted Gross Income		
		Number	Amount	Average	Number	Amount	Average	Number	Amount	Average	Amount	Average	% Sch C
<= 0		772	-3	-3,463	108	6	55,313	666	56	84,075	85	110,094	-3.1%
1	2,500	4,333	-2	-543	381	12	32,413	3,783	222	58,574	290	67,015	-0.8%
2,501	5,000	2,405	3	1,114	215	7	32,944	1,973	108	54,905	147	61,006	1.8%
5,001	10,000	2,572	11	4,164	204	7	33,222	1,845	90	48,797	137	53,256	7.8%
10,001	25,000	1,945	24	12,306	156	6	41,469	962	50	52,318	101	52,039	23.6%
25,001	50,000	329	10	30,445	49	3	57,162	219	18	80,325	40	120,711	25.2%
50,001	100,000	92	6	63,967	16	1	89,873	62	9	141,403	23	247,798	25.8%
100,001	10,000,000	44	9	199,062	14	2	157,765	27	8	296,956	29	668,746	29.8%
TOTAL		12,491	57	4,554	1,143	45	39,480	9,536	561	58,783	852	68,204	6.7%

Table 3: Sensitivity to Business Thresholds
tax year 2007, billions of dollars, thousands of filers

	All Filers	Test 1	Test 2	Test 3	Test 4
1. Income or Deductions >		5,000	10,000	10,000	20,000
2. Sum of Income and Deductions >		7,500	15,000	15,000	30,000
3. Deduction Floor		1,000	1,000	5,000	5,000
Schedule C: Sole Proprietors					
Number of Returns	23,175	13,856	11,667	10,684	8,643
Share of Total Returns	100%	60%	50%	46%	37%
Total Income	1,371	1,320	1,309	1,284	1,259
Share of Total Income	100%	96%	95%	94%	92%
Schedule E: Rent					
Number of Returns	9,636	7,151	5,374	4,593	2,752
Share of Total Returns	100%	74%	56%	48%	29%
Total Income	255	239	228	212	191
Share of Total Income	100%	94%	89%	83%	75%
Schedule F: Farmers					
Number of Returns	2,511	1,794	1,448	1,415	1,017
Share of Total Returns	100%	71%	58%	56%	40%
Total Income	132	130	129	128	126
Share of Total Income	100%	99%	98%	97%	95%
Form 1065: Partnerships					
Number of Returns	3,096	2,463	2,375	2,300	2,166
Share of Total Returns	100%	80%	77%	74%	70%
Total Income	6,172	6,066	6,065	6,048	6,046
Share of Total Income	100%	98%	98%	98%	98%
Form 1120-S: S Corporations					
Number of Returns	3,990	3,689	3,591	3,554	3,408
Share of Total Returns	100%	92%	90%	89%	85%
Total Income	6,302	6,298	6,298	6,295	6,293
Share of Total Income	100%	100%	100%	100%	100%
Form 1120: C Corporations					
Number of Returns	1,865	1,666	1,652	1,638	1,577
Share of Total Returns	100%	89%	89%	88%	85%
Total Income	22,011	22,005	22,005	22,005	22,005
Share of Total Income	100%	100%	100%	100%	100%
TOTAL					
Number of Returns	44,273	30,619	26,108	24,184	19,563
Share of Total Returns	100%	69%	59%	55%	44%
Total Income	36,243	36,059	36,034	35,975	35,919
Share of Total Income	100%	99%	99%	99%	99%

Table 4: Business Versus Small Business Filers
tax year 2007, billions of dollars, thousands of filers

	Number of Filers	Total Income Detail					Net Income Detail			
		Gross Receipts	Gross Rents 1/	Other Income 2/	Total Income	Avg Total Income	Pos Net Income	Neg Net Income	All Net Income	Avg Net Income
Schedule C: Sole Proprietors										
Business	10,684	1,266	na	18	1,284	120,209	268	-45	223	20,854
Small Business	10,679	1,121	na	15	1,136	106,409	265	-43	222	20,742
Schedule E: Rent										
Business	4,593	na	212	na	212	46,238	38	-60	-22	-4,755
Small Business	4,592	na	208	na	208	45,316	38	-59	-21	-4,628
Schedule F: Farmers										
Business	1,415	106	0	25	130	92,194	12	-25	-13	-9,208
Small Business	1,415	100	0	24	125	88,090	12	-25	-13	-9,049
Form 1065: Partnerships										
Business	2,300	3,888	417	1,743	6,048	2,629,841	1,732	-317	1,415	615,282
Small Business	2,232	702	279	182	1,163	521,163	300	-133	167	74,836
Form 1120-S: S Corporations										
Business	3,554	5,973	38	284	6,295	1,770,991	501	-82	419	117,914
Small Business	3,462	2,297	30	90	2,418	698,345	228	-59	169	48,671
Form 1120: C Corporations										
Business	1,638	18,242	102	3,661	22,005	13,433,466	1,305	-247	1,058	646,119
Small Business	1,563	1,336	4	65	1,405	899,097	49	-55	-6	-3,679
TOTALS										
Business	24,184	29,474	769	5,731	35,975	1,487,559	3,857	-776	3,080	127,375
Small Business	23,942	5,557	521	377	6,455	269,601	891	-374	517	21,601

1/ For partnerships and S corporations, includes any gross rents reported on Form 8825.

2/ For partnerships and S corporations, includes all income reported on Schedule K, except net rental real estate income. For partnerships and all corporations, includes net capital gains, dividends, royalties, interest and miscellaneous other income.

Table 5: Small Business Detail by Total Income
tax year 2007, billions of dollars, thousands of filers

Reported Total Income	Number Firms	Total Income Detail					Net Income Detail			
		Gross Receipts	Gross Rents 1/	Other Income 2/	Total Income	Avg Total Income	Pos Net Income	Neg Net Income	All Net Income	Avg Net Income
< 0	132	1	0	-19	-18	-138,765	0	-31	-30	-230,692
0　25,000	8,178	68	38	5	111	13,591	17	-99	-82	-9,985
25,001　50,000	4,220	107	41	5	153	36,204	41	-27	13	3,144
50,001　75,000	2,134	97	31	5	133	62,199	36	-17	18	8,571
75,001　100,000	1,519	113	21	10	144	94,539	36	-14	23	14,858
100,001　250,000	3,432	455	76	27	557	162,353	125	-38	86	25,201
250,001　500,000	1,722	526	64	31	620	360,134	108	-31	77	44,865
500,001　1,000,000	1,173	724	68	43	835	711,842	107	-35	73	61,982
1,000,001　5,000,000	1,244	2,301	150	173	2,623	2,108,715	288	-69	219	175,747
5,000,001　10,000,000	188	1,164	33	99	1,297	6,890,590	133	-13	120	637,992
TOTAL	**23,942**	**5,556**	**521**	**377**	**6,455**	**269,590**	**891**	**-373**	**517**	**21,601**

1/ For partnerships and S corporations, includes any gross rents reported on Form 8825.
2/ For partnerships and S corporations, includes all income reported on Schedule K, except net rental real estate income.
For partnerships and all corporations, includes net capital gains, dividends, royalties, interest and miscellaneous other income.

Table 6: Small Business Detail by Reported Net Income
tax year 2007, billions of dollars, thousands of filers

Reported Net Income		Number Firms	Total Income Detail					Net Income Detail			
			Gross Receipts	Gross Rents 1/	Other Income 2/	Total Income	Avg Total Income	Pos Net Income	Neg Net Income	All Net Income	Avg Net Income
-10,000,000	-1,000,001	44	44	12	-6	50	1,129,172	0	-102	-102	-2,300,062
-1,000,000	-100,001	484	368	58	12	437	904,098	0	-124	-124	-256,042
-100,000	-50,001	589	187	25	5	216	367,586	0	-41	-41	-68,874
-50,000	-1	7,982	705	97	19	822	102,933	0	-107	-107	-13,383
0	25,000	9,315	1,156	70	31	1,258	135,073	85	0	85	9,092
25,001	50,000	2,347	628	35	16	678	288,996	83	0	83	35,437
50,001	100,000	1,578	715	46	19	779	493,652	111	0	111	70,191
100,001	250,000	1,029	818	64	33	914	888,971	159	0	159	154,159
250,001	500,000	327	442	46	34	522	1,596,634	113	0	113	346,191
500,001	1,000,000	139	281	34	35	351	2,530,207	96	0	96	694,560
1,000,001	10,000,000	109	212	35	179	427	3,919,741	244	0	244	2,240,228
TOTAL		**23,942**	**5,556**	**521**	**377**	**6,455**	**269,606**	**891**	**-373**	**517**	**21,607**

1/ For partnerships and S corporations, includes any gross rents reported on Form 8825.

2/ For partnerships and S corporations, includes all income reported on Schedule K, except net rental real estate income.
For partnerships and all corporations, includes net capital gains, dividends, royalties, interest and miscellaneous other income.

28

Table 7: Small Business Detail by Industry
tax year 2007, billions of dollars, thousands of filers

	Number	Total Income Detail					Net Income Detail			
	Firms	Gross Receipts	Gross Rents 1/	Other Income 2/	Total Income	Avg Total Income	Pos Net Income	Neg Net Income	All Net Income	Avg Net Income
Agriculture	1,786	189	2	42	233	130,448	27	-33	-6	-3,487
Mining-Utilities	133	55	0	9	64	483,952	16	-8	8	59,740
Construction	2,609	923	3	13	939	359,866	77	-26	51	19,504
Manufacturing	451	366	0	8	375	831,351	25	-16	9	19,785
Wholesale	538	476	0	9	485	902,227	27	-9	19	34,386
Retail	1,738	859	1	14	874	502,699	38	-20	17	9,835
Transportation	1,019	230	1	7	238	233,676	20	-7	13	12,490
Information	237	79	0	4	83	350,856	10	-10	0	715
Financial	755	184	2	113	299	395,952	121	-31	90	119,527
Real Estate and Rental	7,067	246	509	99	855	120,979	223	-139	84	11,880
Professional and Technical	2,266	619	1	20	639	282,229	133	-25	107	47,287
Administrative and Support	1,010	234	0	5	239	236,764	25	-7	18	18,039
Educational Services	177	22	0	0	23	128,972	3	-1	2	10,108
Health Care and Social Service	1,250	452	1	15	468	374,209	83	-9	74	59,096
Arts and Entertainment	562	83	0	5	88	156,740	14	-8	6	9,950
Accommodation and Food	627	297	1	7	306	487,774	21	-14	7	10,685
All Other Services	1,718	239	0	7	247	143,529	28	-8	20	11,436
TOTAL	**23,942**	**5,556**	**522**	**377**	**6,455**	**269,602**	**891**	**-373**	**517**	**21,600**

1/ For partnerships and S corporations, includes any gross rents reported on Form 8825.

2/ For partnerships and S corporations, includes all income reported on Schedule K, except net rental real estate income.
For partnerships and all corporations, includes net capital gains, dividends, royalties, interest and miscellaneous other income.

29

Table 8: Small Business Employers
tax year 2007, billions of dollars, thousands of filers

	Number Firms	Total Income Detail					Net Income Detail			
		Gross Receipts	Gross Rents 1/	Other Income 2/	Total Income	Avg Total Income	Pos Net Income	Neg Net Income	All Net Income	Avg Net Income
Schedule C: Sole Proprietors										
Employers	1,659	572	0	6	579	348,739	91	-12	79	47,838
Non-Employers	9,020	549	0	9	558	61,833	174	-32	142	15,760
Schedule E: Rent /3										
Employers	0	0	0	0	0	0	0	0	0	0
Non-Employers	4,592	0	208	0	208	45,316	38	-59	-21	-4,628
Schedule F: Farmers										
Employers	126	42	0	10	52	413,932	3	-6	-3	-20,734
Non-Employers	1,289	58	0	15	73	56,342	8	-19	-10	-7,911
Form 1065: Partnerships										
Employers	533	514	102	32	648	1,215,281	92	-47	45	84,395
Non-Employers	1,698	188	177	150	515	303,265	208	-86	122	71,834
Form 1120-S: S Corporations										
Employers	1,760	1,988	11	48	2,047	1,163,103	151	-41	110	62,672
Non-Employers	1,702	309	19	43	371	217,803	77	-18	58	34,178
Form 1120: C Corporations										
Employers	864	1,186	3	42	1,232	1,424,937	33	-41	-8	-9,604
Non-Employers	699	150	1	23	174	248,571	16	-13	3	3,636
TOTAL										
Employers	4,942	4,303	116	138	4,557	922,108	370	-146	224	45,276
Non-Employers	19,000	1,253	406	239	1,898	99,887	520	-227	293	15,442

1/ For partnerships and S corporations, includes any gross rents reported on Form 8825.

2/ For partnerships and S corporations, includes all income reported on Schedule K, except net rental real estate income.
For partnerships and all corporations, includes net capital gains, dividends, royalties, interest and miscellaneous other income.

3/ Schedule E Rental Income filers do not itemize expenses related to the employment of individuals. For the purposes of this table, we count all Schedule E filers as non-employers.

Table 9: Small Business Labor and Depreciation Deductions
tax year 2007, billions of dollars, thousands of filers

Total Income	Number Firms	Wages-Salaries			Compensation of Officers / Guar. Payments to Partners			Depreciation 1/		
		Number	Amount	Average	Number	Amount	Average	Number	Amount	Average
Sole Proprietors										
<= 100,000	8,177	685	7	10,537	na	na	na	3,535	13	3,774
100,001 500,000	2,131	851	39	46,314	na	na	na	1,399	14	10,133
500,001 1,000,000	245	174	25	141,012	na	na	na	190	4	22,428
1,000,001 10,000,000	125	95	34	353,941	na	na	na	102	5	50,544
Total	10,679	1,806	105	58,092	na	na	na	5,226	37	7,069
Partnerships										
<= 100,000	1,000	88	2	26,889	42	1	14,508	217	2	9,749
100,001 500,000	719	224	13	58,068	90	4	41,359	214	3	16,367
500,001 1,000,000	205	110	17	155,958	34	3	86,255	78	2	31,725
1,000,001 10,000,000	307	191	106	556,453	57	15	262,841	145	11	77,941
Total	2,232	613	139	226,423	224	22	99,720	654	19	29,622
S Corporations										
<= 100,000	1,042	247	4	15,142	324	5	16,590	543	3	5,636
100,001 500,000	1,330	828	46	55,460	864	39	44,691	947	11	11,323
500,001 1,000,000	468	409	64	157,081	348	29	82,883	398	9	21,422
1,000,001 10,000,000	622	566	317	559,092	494	88	178,039	555	33	59,493
Total	3,462	2,050	431	210,030	2,031	161	79,187	2,442	55	22,644
C Corporations										
<= 100,000	442	102	4	35,034	102	2	22,129	221	1	6,186
100,001 500,000	535	332	21	63,248	285	16	56,842	363	4	11,592
500,001 1,000,000	220	188	31	162,570	154	18	116,691	181	4	22,642
1,000,001 10,000,000	366	338	216	639,619	285	81	285,213	329	21	63,117
Total	1,563	959	271	282,659	826	118	142,414	1,095	30	27,812
All Small Business Entities										
<= 100,000	10,661	1,122	17	15,059	469	8	17,611	4,517	20	4,403
100,001 500,000	4,715	2,235	119	53,392	1,240	59	47,245	2,923	33	11,155
500,001 1,000,000	1,138	881	137	154,941	536	50	92,785	847	19	22,860
1,000,001 10,000,000	1,421	1,190	673	565,097	836	184	220,348	1,131	70	62,097
Total	17,935	5,428	945	174,175	3,080	301	97,631	9,417	142	15,086

1/ Includes Section 179 expensing.

31

Table 10: Overview of Matches - Number of EINs on INSOLE Schedule E Matched to Partnership and S Corporation Entity Returns on CDW
tax year 2007, unweighted counts

From the Special Schedule E List of EINS	All, Returns or EINS	All Matches		Matches by Type of Entity			Non-matches: EINs not Found on CDW	
	Number (1)	Number (2)	Percent (3)	Partnership (4)	S Corp. (5)	Both (6)	Number (7)	Percent (8)
1040 Returns	126,344							
EINs								
EIN Listings - Total	1,141,963							
Distinct EINS – Total	526,511	493,993	94%	349,403	144,385	205	32,518	6%
EINs Reported on Sch. E as:								
Partnerships	377,609	351,861	93%	347,930	3,857	74	25,748	7%
S Corporations	146,271	139,698	96%	679	138,902	117	6,573	5%
Both	2,631	2,434	93%	794	1,626	14	197	8%

Notes:
EIN = Employer Identification Number
CDW = Compliance Data Warehouse
INSOLE = Individual and Sole Proprietor file

32

Table 11: Ordinary Income of Partners and S Corporation Shareholders - on INSOLE, Schedule E EIN List, and CDW Matches
tax year 2007, billions of dollars, thousands of returns

	Active, Gross Gain		Active, Gross Loss		Passive, Gross Gain		Passive, Gross Loss		Net Income/Loss	
	Returns	Amount	Returns	Amount	Returns	Amount	Returns	Amount	Returns	Amount
Individuals with Partnership Income or Loss 1/ 2/										
INSOLE Returns	1,808	213	1,489	90	1,750	67	1,138	24	4,594	165
CDW match	1,615	193	1,290	77	1,624	61	1,060	21	4,221	156
Match Rate	89%	91%	87%	86%	93%	92%	93%	89%	92%	94%
Individuals with S Corporation Income or Loss 1/ 2/										
INSOLE Returns	2,615	309	1,577	73	578	42	203	5	4,429	273
CDW match	2,473	296	1,439	67	538	40	184	5	4,152	265
Match Rate	95%	96%	91%	92%	93%	94%	91%	89%	94%	97%

1/ Includes returns with any partnership or S corporation EIN with any non-zero amounts in 4 types of income/loss. Exclude EINs where all income/loss pieces = 0.

2/ Total Net Income/Loss is calculated before any deductions for section 179 expensing.

Table 12: Individual Partners and S Corporation Shareholders - Business, Small Business, Employer, Small Employer Income 1/

tax year 2007, billions of dollars, thousands of returns

Individuals with at least one EIN matched to CDW 2/	Partners & S Corporation Shareholders			Partners			S Corporation Shareholders		
	Number Returns	Net Income	Average	Number Returns	Net Income	Average	Number Returns	Net Income	Average
	(1)	(2)	(3)	(4)	(5)	(6)	(7)	(8)	(9)
All Matched 3/	7,452	421	56,458	4,221	155.6	36,862	4,153	265	63,842
Business 4/	6,552	416	63,477	3,529	156.9	44,452	3,715	259	69,722
Small Business	5,964	208	34,865	3,014	71.0	23,555	3,532	137	38,770
Not Small Business	976	208	213,081	753	85.9	113,980	247	122	494,119
Employers	2,847	327	114.789	958	117.5	122,711	2,019	209	103,637
Small Business Employers	2,432	132	54,214	702	37.0	52,745	1,824	95	51,997
Percentages of All Returns with Matched EINs									
Business 4/	88%	99%		84%	101%		89%	98%	
Small Business	80%	49%		71%	46%		85%	52%	
Not Small Business	13%	49%		18%	55%		6%	46%	
Employers	38%	78%		23%	76%		49%	79%	
Small Business Employers	33%	31%		17%	24%		44%	36%	

1/ Net income reflects only what is reported on 1040 Sch. E - ordinary + rental income. Net income on entity tables includes portfolio income. We are not able to identify the size, or in many cases the type, of the business from which individuals receive portfolio income.

2/ Excludes EINs with only zero amounts reported on the taxpayer's Schedule E.

3/ "All Matched" means returns that have at least 1 EIN matched to an entity return on the CDW.

4/ The difference between "All" and "Business" reflects entities that are investment vehicles or conduits, showing little or no business activity of their own. Because individuals may own multiple entities, individuals may fall in both the Small and Not Small Business categories.

Table 13: Partners and S Corporation Shareholders and Income -
Business, Small Business, Employer, Small Employer, by Active/Passive and Gain/Loss 1/
tax year 2007, billions of dollars, thousands of returns

Individuals with EINs matched to CDW 2/	Partners				S Corporation Shareholders			
	Positive Income		Negative Income		Positive Income		Negative Income	
	Returns	Amount	Returns	Amount	Returns	Amount	Returns	Amount
	(1)	(2)	(3)	(4)	(5)	(6)	(7)	(8)
Active								
All	1,615	193	1,290	77	2,473	296	1,439	67
Business	1,409	182	912	62	2,374	289	1,163	62
Small Business	1,119	85	806	42	2,240	168	1,129	45
Not Small Business	322	97	130	20	158	121	41	17
Employers	558	131	226	23	1,321	227	563	43
Small Business Employers	391	47	200	13	1,184	114	530	27
Percentages of All Active								
Business	87%	94%	71%	80%	96%	98%	81%	93%
Small Business	69%	44%	62%	54%	91%	57%	78%	68%
Not Small Business	20%	50%	10%	26%	6%	41%	3%	25%
Employers	35%	68%	18%	30%	53%	77%	39%	64%
Small Business Employers	24%	25%	16%	17%	48%	38%	37%	41%
Passive								
All	1,624	61	1,060	21	538	40	184	5
Business	1,395	55	848	19	394	35	100	3
Small Business	1,193	41	662	14	343	16	93	2
Not Small Business	261	14	247	5	59	19	9	1
Employers	188	13	117	3	231	27	54	2
Small Business Employers	111	4	75	2	179	10	47	1
Percentages of All Passive								
Business	86%	90%	80%	87%	73%	87%	55%	71%
Small Business	73%	67%	62%	64%	64%	40%	50%	47%
Not Small Business	16%	23%	23%	23%	11%	47%	5%	24%
Employers	12%	21%	11%	15%	43%	68%	29%	47%
Small Business Employers	7%	7%	7%	8%	33%	24%	25%	25%

1/ Net income reflects only what is reported on 1040 Sch. E - ordinary + rental income. Net income on earlier tables includes portfolio income. We are not able to identify the size, or in many cases the type, of the business from which individuals receive portfolio income.
2/ Includes only EINs with some non-zero amounts reported on the taxpayer's Schedule E. Individuals may own multiple types of businesses.

Table 14: Distribution of Individual Tax Returns - All, with Any Flow-Through Income, and with Small Business Income, by AGI

tax year 2007, billions of dollars, thousands of returns

Adjusted Gross Income (AGI)	All Tax Returns				With Any Flow-Through Income 1/				Business Owners 2/			
	Number Returns	Percent Total	AGI	Percent Total	Number Returns	Percent Total	Flow-Through Income	Percent Total	Number Returns	Percent Total	Business Income	Percent Total
Under $0	1,476	1%	-110	-1%	1,149	3%	-73	-11%	988	5%	-63	-11%
0 - 50,000	92,275	65%	1,949	22%	16,714	48%	74	11%	8,566	42%	44	8%
50,000 100,000	31,185	22%	2,209	25%	8,729	25%	63	10%	5,063	25%	54	9%
100,000 200,000	13,505	9%	1,800	21%	5,259	15%	98	15%	3,489	17%	86	15%
200,000 500,000	3,494	2%	1,005	12%	2,066	6%	148	22%	1,732	8%	136	23%
500,000 1 million	651	0%	442	5%	491	1%	94	14%	447	2%	87	15%
$1 million +	392	0%	1,401	16%	331	1%	258	39%	311	2%	237	41%
ALL	**142,979**	**100%**	**8,695**	**100%**	**34,740**	**100%**	**662**	**100%**	**20,596**	**100%**	**581**	**100%**
Addendum:												
Over $200,000	4,538	3%	2,848	33%	2,888	8%	500	75%	2,490	12%	460	79%
Over $500,000	1,043	1%	1,843	21%	822	2%	352	53%	758	4%	324	56%

Adjusted Gross Income (AGI)	Small Business Owners - Broad Definition 3/				Small Business Owners - Narrow Definition 4/				Owners of Any Larger Business 5/			
	Number Returns	Percent Total	Small Business Income	Percent Total	Number Returns	Percent Total	Small Business Income	Percent Total	Number of Returns	Percent Total	Large Business Income	Percent Total
Under $0	983	5%	-48	-13%	670	7%	-38	-11%	24	2%	-15	-7%
0 - 50,000	8,466	42%	45	12%	5,388	57%	51	15%	146	12%	0	0%
50,000 100,000	4,948	25%	54	14%	1,633	17%	55	16%	196	16%	0	0%
100,000 200,000	3,341	17%	83	22%	991	11%	76	23%	268	22%	2	1%
200,000 500,000	1,606	8%	117	31%	540	6%	99	30%	295	24%	19	9%
500,000 1 million	399	2%	58	15%	116	1%	45	13%	144	12%	29	14%
$1 million +	273	1%	67	18%	51	1%	47	14%	166	13%	170	83%
ALL	**20,016**	**100%**	**376**	**100%**	**9,390**	**100%**	**335**	**100%**	**1,240**	**100%**	**205**	**100%**
Addendum:												
Over $200,000	2,278	11%	242	64%	707	8%	191	57%	606	49%	218	106%
Over $500,000	672	3%	125	33%	167	2%	92	27%	310	25%	199	97%

1/ Includes income or loss from Sch. C, E-rental, F, and partnership and S corporation income as reported on Sch. E part II.

2/ Individuals with income or loss from any flow-through entity meeting the definition of a "business."

3/ Individuals with income or loss from any business that meets the definition of a "small business."

4/ Only individuals with active net income from small businesses that equals at least 25 percent of the taxpayer's AGI.

5/ Owners of any entity that meets the definition of "business" but that is not a small business. Some owners of large businesses also own small businesses and are considered "small business owners." Income of small businesses and income of larger businesses are only reported in their respective categories.

Table 15: Employers by AGI - Returns with Any Flow-through Income, with Income from Employer Businesses, and with Income from Small Business Employers

tax year 2007, billions of dollars, thousands of returns

Adjusted Gross Income (AGI)	With Any Flow-Through Income 1/				With Employer Business Income 2/				With Small Employer Business Income 3/			
	Number of Returns	Percent Total	Flow-Through Income	Percent Total	Number Returns	Percent Total	Employer Income	Percent Total	Number Returns	Percent Total	Small Employer Income	Percent Total
Under $0	1,149	3%	-73	-11%	239	6%	-28	-7%	231	6%	-18	-10%
0 - 50,000	16,714	48%	74	11%	1,025	24%	7	2%	994	26%	7	4%
50,000 - 100,000	8,729	25%	63	10%	920	22%	17	5%	861	23%	17	9%
100,000 - 200,000	5,259	15%	98	15%	887	21%	40	11%	799	21%	37	20%
200,000 - 500,000	2,066	6%	148	22%	750	18%	87	23%	617	16%	68	37%
500,000 - 1 million	491	1%	94	14%	251	6%	65	17%	180	5%	37	20%
$1 million +	331	1%	258	39%	200	5%	189	50%	126	3%	35	19%
ALL	**34,740**	**100%**	**662**	**100%**	**4,272**	**100%**	**376**	**100%**	**3,808**	**100%**	**183**	**100%**
Addendum:												
Over $200,000	2,888	8%	500	75%	1,201	28%	341	91%	923	24%	140	76%
Over $500,000	822	2%	352	53%	451	11%	254	67%	306	8%	72	39%

1/ Includes income or loss from Sch. C, E-rental, F, and partnership and S corporation income as reported on Sch. E part II.
2/ From businesses meeting the definition of "employer."
3/ From businesses meeting the definitions of "employer" and "small."

Table 16: Sources of Income for Small Business Owners (Broad and Narrow Definitions) and Small Business Employers, by AGI Class

tax year 2007, billions of dollars, thousands of returns

AGI Class	Number Owners	Share of Total 2/	Sole Prop	Rent & Farm	S Corp	P'ship	Total Bus Inc	Share of Total	Wages-Salaries 1/	Net Cap Gains	Int & Divs	Other 2/	Total Income 2/	Share of Total
Broad Definition of Small Business Owners 2/														
Under $0	983	5%	-9	-12	-14	-13	-48	-13%	12	13	7	-77	-93	-3%
0 - 50,000	8,466	42%	53	-13	1	3	45	12%	119	6	8	33	211	7%
50,000 100,000	4,948	25%	47	-9	11	6	54	14%	228	14	12	65	373	13%
100,000 200,000	3,341	17%	52	-5	23	13	83	22%	266	31	16	82	478	17%
200,000 500,000	1,606	8%	50	1	42	24	117	31%	228	58	19	73	495	18%
500,000 1 million	399	2%	15	1	26	16	58	15%	106	55	13	47	279	10%
$1 million +	273	1%	13	3	32	19	67	18%	217	475	66	250	1,075	38%
TOTAL	20,016	100%	222	-34	121	67	376	100%	1,176	652	141	474	2,818	100%
Broad Definition of Small Business Owners 2/ - EMPLOYERS														
Under $0	231	6%	-4	-1	-9	-4	-18	-10%	6	8	5	-48	-48	-5%
0 - 50,000	994	26%	7	0	-1	1	7	4%	17	1	1	2	29	3%
50,000 100,000	861	23%	10	0	4	2	17	9%	38	3	2	7	67	7%
100,000 200,000	799	21%	17	0	13	7	37	20%	57	7	4	15	121	12%
200,000 500,000	617	16%	23	0	31	14	68	37%	75	19	7	28	197	19%
500,000 1 million	180	5%	7	0	20	9	37	20%	41	21	6	22	126	12%
$1 million +	126	3%	5	-1	24	6	35	19%	85	249	38	130	536	52%
TOTAL	3,808	100%	66	-1	83	35	183	100%	319	308	63	155	1,029	100%
Narrow Definition of Small Business Owners 3/														
Under $0	670	7%	-9	-4	-13	-12	-38	-11%	9	7	4	-21	-39	-5%
0 - 50,000	5,388	57%	52	-4	1	2	51	15%	54	3	3	10	122	17%
50,000 100,000	1,633	17%	44	-1	8	4	55	16%	52	5	3	12	127	18%
100,000 200,000	991	11%	49	0	17	9	76	23%	47	8	4	15	150	21%
200,000 500,000	540	6%	47	0	36	17	99	30%	43	11	5	14	173	24%
500,000 1 million	116	1%	14	0	21	10	45	13%	18	9	3	7	82	11%
$1 million +	51	1%	11	0	27	9	47	14%	15	21	7	13	102	14%
TOTAL	9,390	100%	208	-8	97	39	335	100%	238	64	30	50	716	100%

Column groups: "Sources of Net Small Business Income" covers Sole Prop, Rent & Farm, S Corp, P'ship, Total Bus Inc, Share of Total. "Sources of Total Income 1/" covers Wages-Salaries 1/, Net Cap Gains, Int & Divs, Other 2/, Total Income 2/, Share of Total.

1/ Total Income includes small business income. "Wages-salaries" could include officer compensation for S corporation owners. "Other Income" includes flow-through income from entities that do not meet the small business definition.

2/ Broad definition of small business owner includes any individual taxpayer with any income or loss from a business that meets our definition of a "small business."

3/ Narrow definition of small business owner includes only individuals with active net income from small businesses that equals at least 25% of the taxpayer's AGI.

Table 17: Distribution of Individual Tax Returns with Positive Taxable Income by Statutory Marginal Tax Rate 1/ and Type of Income

tax year 2007, billions of dollars, thousands of returns

All Tax Returns

Statutory Marginal Tax Rate 1/	Number Returns	Percent Total	AGI	Percent Total
10%	27,575	25%	554	7%
15%	50,542	46%	2,362	28%
25%	23,547	21%	2,109	25%
28%	3,692	3%	565	7%
33%	512	0%	134	2%
35%	679	1%	1,242	15%
AMT 26%	1,164	1%	154	2%
AMT 28%	2,996	3%	1,376	16%
ALL	110,707	100%	8,497	100%
Addendum:				
33 & 35% rates	1,191	1%	1,376	16%

With Any Flow-Through Inc. 1/

Statutory Marginal Tax Rate 1/	Number Returns	Percent Total	Flow-Through Income	Percent Total
10%	4,676	18%	22	3%
15%	10,498	41%	63	9%
25%	6,144	24%	78	11%
28%	1,408	5%	44	6%
33%	302	1%	25	4%
35%	521	2%	329	47%
AMT 26%	486	2%	9	1%
AMT 28%	1,849	7%	136	19%
ALL	25,884	100%	705	100%
Addendum:				
33 & 35% rates	823	3%	353	50%

Business Owners 2/

Statutory Marginal Tax Rate 1/	Number Returns	Percent Total	Business Income	Percent Total
10%	2,628	17%	16	2%
15%	5,759	37%	53	8%
25%	3,639	23%	67	11%
28%	1,008	6%	39	6%
33%	249	2%	22	4%
35%	481	3%	301	48%
AMT 26%	357	2%	8	1%
AMT 28%	1,580	10%	127	20%
ALL	15,701	100%	632	100%
Addendum:				
33 & 35% rates	730	5%	323	51%

Owners of Any Larger Business 5/

Statutory Marginal Tax Rate 1/	Number Returns	Percent Total	Larger Business Income	Percent Total
10%	40	3%	0	0%
15%	165	14%	0	0%
25%	234	20%	1	0%
28%	108	9%	2	1%
33%	32	3%	2	1%
35%	198	17%	188	85%
AMT 26%	34	3%	1	0%
AMT 28%	360	31%	27	12%
ALL	1,171	100%	220	100%
Addendum:				
33 & 35% rates	230	20%	190	86%

Small Bus. Owners - Broad 3/

Statutory Marginal Tax Rate 1/	Number Returns	Percent Total	Small Business Income	Percent Total
10%	2,604	17%	16	4%
15%	5,659	37%	53	13%
25%	3,494	23%	67	16%
28%	947	6%	37	9%
33%	237	2%	20	5%
35%	422	3%	113	27%
AMT 26%	344	2%	7	2%
AMT 28%	1,441	10%	100	24%
ALL	15,148	100%	412	100%
Addendum:				
33 & 35% rates	659	4%	133	32%

Small Bus. Owners-Narrow 4/

Statutory Marginal Tax Rate 1/	Number Returns	Percent Total	Small Business Income	Percent Total
10%	1,522	26%	17	5%
15%	2,236	38%	55	15%
25%	1,027	18%	62	17%
28%	304	5%	33	9%
33%	103	2%	18	5%
35%	136	2%	86	24%
AMT 26%	96	2%	6	2%
AMT 28%	403	7%	78	22%
ALL	5,828	100%	356	100%
Addendum:				
33 & 35% rates	239	4%	105	29%

1/ The statutory marginal tax rate is the statutory rate applicable to the last dollar of taxable income.
2/ Includes income or loss from Sch. C, E-rental, F, and partnership and S corporation income as reported on Sch. E part II.
3/ Any individuals with income or loss from any business that meets the definition of a "small business."
4/ Only individuals with active net income from small businesses that equals at least 25% of taxpayer's AGI.
5/ Owners of any entities that meet the definition of "business" but that are not small businesses. Some also own small business and are considered "small business owners." Income of small businesses and income of larger businesses are only reported in their respective categories.

Table 18: Employers by Statutory Marginal Tax Rate 1/ - Returns with Positive Taxable Income and Any Flow-through Income, Income from Employer Businesses, and Income from Small Business Employers

tax year 2007, billions of dollars, thousands of returns

Statutory Marginal Tax Rate 1/	With Any Flow-Through Income 2/				With Employer Business Income 3/				With Small Employer Business Income 4/			
	Number Returns	Percent Total	Flow-Through Income	Percent Total	Number Returns	Percent Total	Employer Income	Percent Total	Number Returns	Percent Total	Employer Income	Percent Total
10%	4,676	18%	22	3%	352	10%	4	1%	341	11%	4	2%
15%	10,498	41%	63	9%	926	26%	16	4%	884	28%	16	8%
25%	6,144	24%	78	11%	753	21%	26	6%	681	22%	25	13%
28%	1,408	5%	44	6%	299	8%	20	5%	265	8%	19	9%
33%	302	1%	25	4%	113	3%	13	3%	97	3%	11	6%
35%	521	2%	329	47%	309	9%	235	58%	204	7%	66	33%
AMT 26%	486	2%	9	1%	114	3%	5	1%	101	3%	4	2%
AMT 28%	1,849	7%	136	19%	701	20%	85	21%	550	18%	57	28%
ALL	**25,884**	**100%**	**705**	**100%**	**3,569**	**100%**	**404**	**100%**	**3,123**	**100%**	**201**	**100%**
Addendum:												
33 & 35%	823	3%	353	50%	423	12%	249	61%	302	10%	77	38%

1/ The statutory rate is the rate applicable to the last dollar of taxable income.
2/ Includes income or loss from Sch. C, E-rental, F, and partnership and S corporation income as reported on Sch. E part II.
3/ From businesses meeting the definition of "employer."
4/ From businesses meeting the definitions of "employer" and "small."